## A SPICY AND OPINIONATED HERB BOOK

For those who are alarmed by the pollution, cancers and poisons of our technological age, this book indicates a road back to sanity through the use of natural food and herbs and a simple technique of self-awareness.

# A SPICY AND OPINIONATED HERB BOOK

*by*

**Joanne Bylsma-Vriens**
Illustrations by Ko van den Broecke

THORSONS PUBLISHERS LIMITED
Wellingborough, Northamptonshire

Published in Holland as *een kruid-ig en eigen-wijs boekje*

First published in England 1977



ISBN 0 7225 0385 7

Photoset by
Specialised Offset Services Ltd., Liverpool
and printed and bound in Great Britain by
Weatherby Woolnough, Wellingborough, Northants

# CONTENTS

To my Mother

# FOREWORD

Lengthy books on dietetics are of no benefit to housewives who have little time to sit down and read. And, nine times out of ten, if cookery books are given as presents they will never leave the bookcase because the busy housewife has little inclination to measure everything out in ounces or grammes. She prefers to do the cooking by instinct.

All the same, if she hears of some new dish discovered by the lady down the road she will want to try it out. This is only human nature, and it is why housewives will at least be keen to read this book by Joanne Bylsma-Vriens. It is written in a lively chatty way with lots of good advice and new ideas which will break through the humdrum cookery routine. It reveals how simple living can be once our eyes are opened to what Mother Nature has left growing on our doorsteps.

Everything mentioned in this book can be grown in your own garden, or obtained from the local greengrocer or health food shop. There is nothing exotic and unobtainable to dampen the reader's enthusiasm. Joanne's suggestions can be put into practice immediately, and family meals which may have become monotonous will gain a new relish and be welcomed with enthusiasm.

The disappearance of a lot of your health problems is an added bonus which will bring extra delight after a few months. Nature protects, nourishes and blesses the individual who gratefully accepts what grows and uses it straight from the soil without any artificial processing.

MELLIE UYLDERT
Dietitian and Herbalist

CHAPTER ONE

# COOKING IS MY WATCHWORD

Whenever I try to put pen to paper, I am seized by a fit of discouragement because I cannot think how to begin. I fidget uneasily in my chair for a while and then, more often than not, return to the kitchen and start cooking.

Cooking is one of the most constructive occupations I know and it will always interest me; not on account of the tasty morsels which may be concocted, the subtle flavours or the marvellous aromas which hang over the stove, and not because it is a game for finding new ways to tickle the palate or to stuff the body with food it could well do without. No, for me, cooking (and everything to do with eating) is a search for balance and harmony, both mental and physical. You may raise your eyebrows as you read this, but nevertheless it is true.

Our homely, everyday eating three times a day requires a certain amount of time and trouble and a certain amount of effort in going shopping, plus insight and a knowledge of foodstuffs; and yet, how often everything connected with it is performed in a perfunctory manner, simply because the present generation has no time to spare, or no time it wants to spare.

Compelled by the pressures in favour of efficiency and by the need to earn money, people leave their houses to toil for the pretty things which make life more agreeable and for the expensive machines which make it less tiring, with the result that no one has time to do anything for themselves and machines are urgently needed to take over the work. Industry has eagerly seized on this state of affairs and has produced clever ready-to-use packets which persuade people that pre-packed meals are their birthright and that home cooking is a waste of time.

Consequently we are caught up in a vicious circle of work, money, machines, convenience and free time. Free time at first hearing sounds like a recipe for endless delight; but what pleasure is left when there is nothing but unceasing idleness?

## WIDESPREAD DISSATISFACTION

We have all the possessions we want, or are busy acquiring them, and yet very few people feel *ful*filled. Their lives are *over* full, and they themselves are restless, empty, nervy and discontented. We realize that with our high standard of living and the benefits of the welfare state, we ought to be satisfied, but never has dissatisfaction been more widespread. This is partly due to the fact that people end up with nothing they need to do and have been deprived of the joy of creativity. Our economic system has been carried to such an extreme that each of us is detailed to make one cog in some mysterious wheel which probably we shall never see. We make our cog in order to earn our wage packet, but can hardly feel any satisfaction in the process.

Opportunities of producing an article in its entirety are few and far between; that would cost too much time and money and would waste valuable energy besides.

Things have gone so far with our menfolk as to pose a serious threat to health. They suffer from executive diseases, cardiac and circulatory conditions, hernias and what not. We see that something is wrong but can do nothing about it – nothing except offer medical help and keep our fingers crossed. If matters do not turn out as well as expected, there are impatient youngsters waiting to step into the breach. Things are always waiting to be changed.

The female section of the population is in an even worse plight. Once again in our economy everything is expected to become more strenuous and more efficient, to keep affairs running properly. Staying at home and making things is unfashionable: it is out of step with the modern world. Industry can now do what the housewife used to do, and can do it better and cheaper than she did. And everything that can be done better and cheaper is so much time saved, time which can be spent in taking part in the production process.

In one generation we shall reach the point where women lose their present advantage of living longer on average than men. They too will be subject to a high incidence of cardiac and circulatory disorders, nerve troubles and hernias. As soon as we have chained them to the health-sapping, deadening treadmill of the conveyor belt, they too will become victims of the monster we know as the 'welfare' state.

**MY PERSONAL ANSWER**

Do not look to me for any solutions. I know of

no better way out than you do, though all of us must have given the subject some thought. However, I have in fact found my own personal answer, as a means of letting off steam. You have already guessed it – cooking is my watchword. To you it may seem naïve, but not to me. Cooking, kitchen gardening and all that goes with them have a more far-reaching influence than you might imagine. The person who feeds with deliberate intent knows what he or she is buying and why. An individual who eats what nature provides for us ready to hand, can keep himself healthy, attractive-looking and fit long after others of his age have become withered and feeble.

CHAPTER TWO

# HOME-MADE BREAD AND MUESLI

One need not suffer from shattered nerves, worn out by living, if one knows the ABC of a sensible diet, and above all if one knows oneself. Coming to know ourselves engenders an instinctive sense of what may be done, eaten or worn. 'Know thyself' – it seems so simple, but is extremely difficult. It demands 'fine tuning', to pick up one's innermost voice.

You had this voice when you were a small child, when you accepted or rejected food intuitively and liked to make-believe, perhaps, that household objects were your friends or that you could talk to fairies.

We have to recover something of this state of mind, and when we do we shall discard much that is superfluous. Auto-intoxication affects us much more radically than we tend to think. However, within a few months of eating very simply you will become so much more healthy and clear-headed that you will have a new capacity for living and be bursting with all sorts of plans and ideas.

Fairly simple meals are certainly not condemned to be dull, far from it. Carefully prepared meals will strike no one as simple. On the other hand, everything redundant is ruthlessly cut out, and so are precooked and prepacked foods.

## BAKING YOUR OWN BREAD

You will be doing everything for yourself again, even baking your own bread; there is no doubt about it, it is twenty-five times tastier and fifty times better than all the overdone, puffed-up bakery loaves put together. Does it strike you as quite a daunting enterprise? Do you fancy it would be too hard to do and that, anyway, the food manufacturers do it so much better? Such an attitude is merely the result of clever indoctrination by these very manufacturers, in their attempt to win a monopoly. At this rate, peeling and boiling our own potatoes and cleaning fresh greens for the pot will soon become a thing of the past.

All of a sudden housework has become too difficult, or so they say, and, if it is repeated long enough, the housewife with this idea lodged in her head will really become incapable of doing anything about the home. Dismiss it from your mind. Baking bread is no more difficult than cooking potatoes, which is something we all do as a matter of course.

What you will need is a bread tin (or a cake tin will do). Buy 4 oz. (100g) fresh yeast from your baker; keep out about ½ oz. (15g) – this will be enough for one loaf – and put the remainder in the fridge until next time.

Mix the ½ oz. yeast with a little lukewarm milk and add a teaspoonful of brown sugar or a teaspoonful of honey. When this has risen add a ½ pint (¼l) of water, ½ lb (225g) of flour and a handful of bran (from a health food shop). Now stir for a few minutes and, when everything is well mixed, add another ½ lb of flour with a pinch of salt and knead thoroughly by hand for five minutes. Tap the side of the mixing bowl once or twice to enable easy removal of the beautifully springy pliable dough, and transfer it to the baking tin, leave in a warm place for about a quarter of an hour.

When the dough has risen put it into the oven at Gas No. 8/450°F (230°C) for half an hour. You now have a glorious loaf of bread, and a hot oven which I usually take advantage of by making an apple pie or rice pudding.

What a sight – such bread! What satisfaction and above all what a delicious smell in the house! Hard work? After a little experience, it will become automatic. It just has to be learnt like any other form of cookery.

When you have the making of this particular loaf at your fingertips and it slips effortlessly from the tin two or three times a week, you will naturally be tempted to try variations. So mix in a handful of barley meal or Sesame seed, some rye-flour or buckwheat; and you can also make gingerbread and currant loaf. You can try baking a wholemeal loaf or nut bread. The mouthwatering variations are too many to mention.

These loaves will now appear in your simple breakfast menus, one of which is based on bread and butter, the other on muesli. Muesli is something else which is very simple to prepare, besides being exceptionally good for you.

## MAKING YOUR OWN MUESLI

Visit the health food store and purchase a bag of rolled oatflakes and a bag of flaked barley. At night, before going to bed, soak about 3 tablespoonsful of oatflakes per person in a little water. Next morning add 3 soupspoonsful of flaked barley, a handful of washed raisins, a coarse-grated large apple, a banana, a tablespoonful of honey, some nuts or sunflower seeds, the juice of half a lemon and a dash of cream from the top of the milk bottle. It is easy to make but it will sustain you all morning. It is amazing how nourishing muesli is and how delicious. Those who still feel hungry can be given a slice of ryebread and a lump of cheese but it really is not necessary. For the time being then, this is what you have for breakfast: home-baked bread and muesli.

## CHAPTER THREE

# 'MEAL-TIME' IS 'MILL-TIME'

Your lunches will be a revelation, for twice a week they will consist of fruit: an apple, a pear, half a grapefruit, nuts, raisins, a banana, a few dried apricots which have been left to soak. Is this too little? Definitely not, but for your husband or others who like to feel 'full', provide a piece of crispbread with cheese and a glass of milk.

On other days eat more of your home-made bread but, please, not peppered with sugar crystals or candied caraway seeds. Put apple on your slice, or cucumber, radish, yeast extract with black radish, tomato, banana, figs, nuts or home-made jam.

Home-made jam is so marvellous that you will become an enthusiast for it, and there is the further advantage that – as the maker – you will know just what is in it. Typical recipes are for tomato and ginger, tomato and lemon, elderberry, apricot. Two or three jars of each sort should be enough; it is pointless to make more than you know what to do with and tedious too. The morning is a good time to make your jam, when you are fresh. It will only take an hour to make a couple of jars and, before you know it, you will have a stock of twelve – quite enough to see you through the winter.

**BENEFITS OF CHEWING**

Your cooking will be flavoured with yeast extract and garnished with the chives or parsley, and you will rediscover chervil and garden cress. This involves a little more trouble than tipping frozen peas into boiling water, but the result is a good deal more inviting. But mind you chew everything well, otherwise all your trouble will be wasted. If you do not learn how to chew you might as well not bother, but continue eating as you have always done – there is no help for you. No stomach or intestines can tolerate a procession of lumps and pieces. The individual who does not masticate his food properly will make himself ill sooner or later.

Chewing has the further benefit of bringing out the taste of the food; especially the taste of that home-made bread which simply begs to be chewed. The less mastication there is, the less saliva is mixed with the food; but the alimentary canal is so designed that the process of digestion begins in the mouth. What is more, we have thirty-two teeth which must be exercised regularly if we are not going to lose them. Think of 'meal-time' as 'mill-time' and set your molars milling away!

Saliva is a digestive ferment of the first order (every child knows how to remove stains with spittle). So digestion starts in the mouth and what happens there sets its mark on the whole digestive process. Furthermore, it is the only part of that process on which a person can exercise a direct influence. Once we have swallowed, we must leave digestion to our insides. Nevertheless, sluggish bowels are the fault of inefficient chewing. We burden our lymph and blood vessels with work we could be doing with our teeth, and hinder them from doing their own work. The result is constipation with straining at the stool, or no motions at all, and on top of that piles (haemorrhoids) and stomach-ache.

# CHAPTER FOUR

# NETTLES, DANDELION AND SORREL

By this time you may be finding yourself rather busier than you used to be, but at least the work makes good sense, which is more than can be said of every job. We are now well on our way. In fact it does not seem like a way any more; you must admit how inspiring and interesting it is. You feel energetic and occupied and I do not think it will be too troublesome to go on further.

## INDISPENSABLE STINGING NETTLES

Very good, that is what we shall do. We shall now see what can be made of the main meal, which will soon no longer consist of thick soups, fancy sausages, indigestible meat dishes and titbits. You will learn to appreciate special flavours like those of carrot salad and celeriac, light broths and natural herbs. You will have the pleasure of going out to find what nature has in store for you, and that is a lot more than you might realize. How long is it since you have eaten stinging nettles? Have you ever realized how good they are for you? If not, that is a pity. Not only are they delicious, and I do mean delicious; they are indispensable. They are rich in protein and contain potassium, calcium, sodium, iron, manganese, sulphur, chlorine,

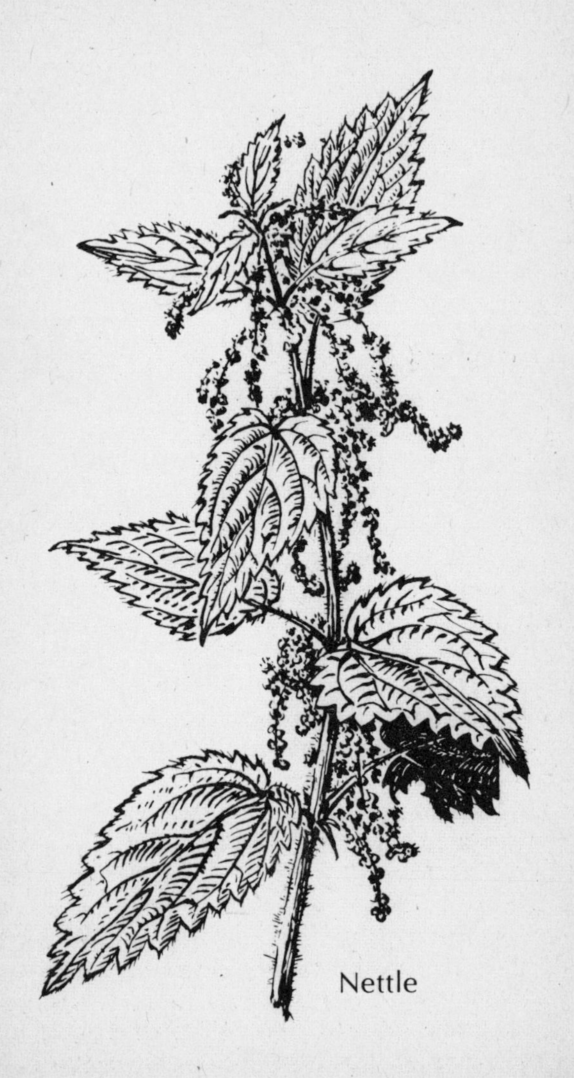

Nettle

magnesium and vitamin A. Quite a list is it not? Hardly credible, and all found in a 'weed'. As you see, we shall do well to abandon the derogatory term 'weed'.

The stinging nettle assists the removal of excess water and the waste products of metabolism, thus purifying the blood. It frees your blood of the surplus 'rubbish' with which it has been loaded due to faulty mastication among other things. Nettles in spring, when they are still young and tender, are an ideal supplement to the diet after a winter of kale and meat stew.

Put on a pair of gloves (although this is not really necessary in early spring) and pick the tops, steeping them for some five minutes in hot water to get rid of the 'sting'. Then drop a generous chopped handful (exactly as if it were chervil) into some stock and you will have a month's eating of a regular and glorious spring soup which is invaluable. I hasten to add that if you do not like it you can 'have your money back', as the saying is, for there are very few people who do not appreciate this soup. However, it is a good policy not to tell the fastidious members of your family what sort of greens they are eating the first time; let the secret wait until after they have enjoyed them. Above all, take plenty of this soup to make you feel like a new person and avoid spring tiredness. You should enjoy it so much that it will quickly establish itself as a firm favourite. So, every spring make stinging nettle soup for a month, or take it chopped up raw on bread and butter with perhaps a scraping of yeast extract to enhance the flavour.

## DANDELION ERADICATES NERVOUS TENSION

And then go and look for a dandelion leaf. Have you forgotten that this is another edible plant? As long as dandelions are growing out-of-doors, the tranquillizers can be left where they are in the medicine chest. It is wonderful what this herb will do for you. It completely eradicates nervous tension. The leaf contains calcium, manganese (restlessness and anxiety often indicate a manganese deficiency), de-acidifying sodium, blood-cleansing sulphur and silicic acid, in addition to saponin which promotes the assimilation of calcium. Excess fluid is eliminated to restore slimness, and piles (haemorrhoids) disappear thanks to an improved circulation.

These are all good reasons for trying the virtues of the forgotten and neglected dandelion. It is hard to credit that some people dare not or will not eat it. A multitude of assorted tablets can stay in their bottles when the dandelion is rehabilitated. Certainly, it tastes bitter, but bitters are good for the heart (and this is no old wives' fable). Anyway, a few leaves mixed into a cabbage and lettuce salad give it a nutty taste.

Pick a leaf or two in the nearest piece of waste ground and chew it up. It is no more odd or unhygienic to do this than to pick a fresh tomato and eat it, and quite as beneficial. Pick some waybread (plantain) too. This is impossible to overlook because the leaf spreads out over everything. It is very rich it vitamin C and costs nothing. Chew a leaf every day, or cut up two or three leaves with the dandelion you put in your

Dandelion

cabbage and lettuce salad. It will keep you fit and well. Children will welcome it as they do anything new and interesting. The chances are they will like it too and begin to glow with health – a glow which can positively be seen, like the shine on the fur of a well-fed dog. And as for your husband, if you serve the salad in glass dishes with radishes or cucumber, cress or tomatoes, he will like the look of it, and if you put it in front of him without comment will probably notice nothing out of the way. Then, as his waistline gets slimmer and daily bowel motions are no longer a misery, he will be grateful. A lot depends on how much attention you pay to food presentation. The salad varieties suggested here can look just as tempting as an ordinary salad and at least as tasty.

## SORREL NEUTRALIZES OXALIC ACID

Is all this new to you? Most people know nothing about it now, although once it was common knowledge and there is no reason why it should not become so again. Your grandparents were better informed. They used to shop for sorrel (*Rumex acetosa*), which went so indispensably with spinach and now is universally forgotten. And did you know that sorrel has been replaced by eggs and that eggs are not merely a pretty decoration for the spinach tin, but necessary to neutralize the harmful oxalic acid?

Nowadays, young people, imagine that it is a package designer's fad, but in that case the same 'decoration' might just as well be used with endives or peas. No, the eggs have a definite purpose in that they counteract the loss of calcium due to the oxalic acid in spinach. Have you ever eaten sorrel stew with raisins and brown sugar? It's just as nice as rhubarb and also very tasty, a delicacy for those who are prepared to try something new.

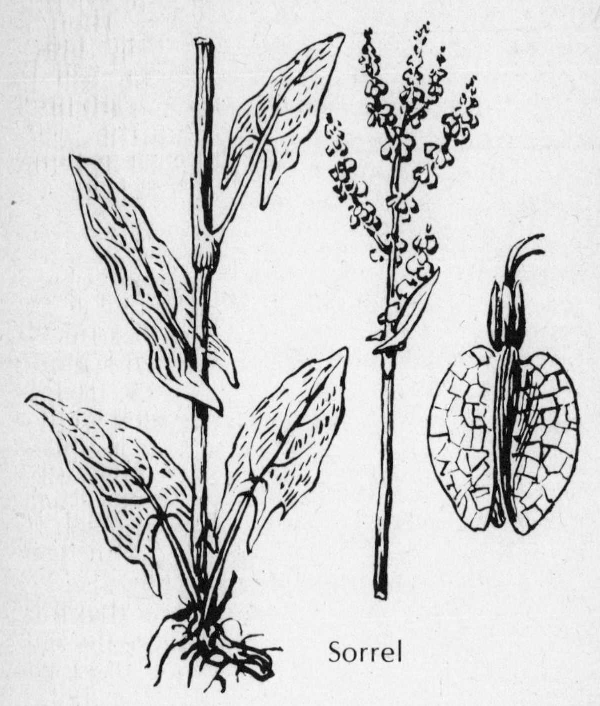

Sorrel

We have already mentioned the egg, but do you use all of it? There is no better source of calcium than egg shells, and it is free too. You peel off the shell and grind it up fine in a mill (I myself employ a hand-turned coffee mill), and then put it through the big mixer with a dash of milk. (My dog gets some sprinkled over his brown bread crumble).

CHAPTER FIVE

# FORGOTTEN HERBS

Now you have already eaten three unlikely things and enjoyed them. You are just as ready to use them as you were with paprika and garlic some years ago, which are now indispensable to you. No wonder, either, for paprika contains a splendid quantity of vitamin C and garlic has no equal as a cleanser of the walls of the veins.

So by now you are gradually becoming convinced, that is if you have not dismissed what I have written with a shrug of your shoulders. You could do this of course and fall back on the old wisecrack that you are no rabbit, but that would be rather short-sighted of you, since rabbits, in common with other wild animals, know what they should eat and when. Only man has lost the instinct. Only man doses himself with endless pills and powders to get rid of stomach ache, headache and so on. A little thought and insight should reveal to you a far more natural way of relieving these pains, but then you must be prepared to set out on the road which lies before you.

## GROW YOUR OWN HERBS

What you are going to do is to restore the old and well-known plants which no one seems to sell any more and the use of which everyone has forgotten. Not only parsley, cress and celery, for these are in common use, but also neglected herbs such as savory, dill, marjoram,

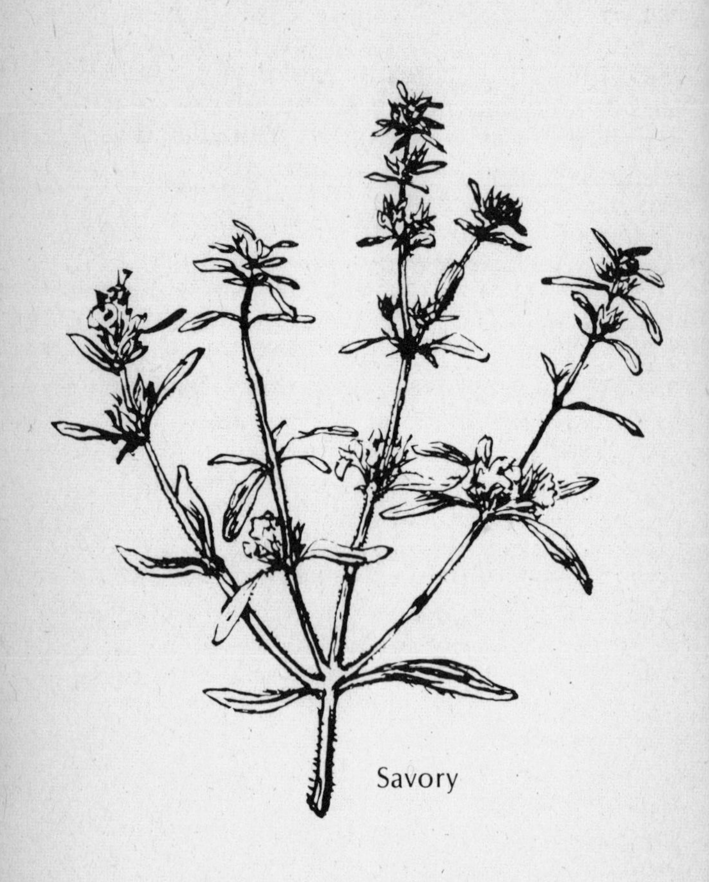

Savory

thyme, sage, burnet, tarragon, basil and fennel, all of which have their uses. They have all been left out of the reckoning because nobody knows what they are good for any more and nobody enquiries. Since the greengrocer cannot or will not sell them, we shall have to grow them in pots standing on the window-sill. It is not hard to do.

More mess, do you say? Yes, in one respect it is I suppose, but children make a mess and so do cats and dogs and, in general, so does anything that lives and grows. However, looked at another way, it becomes a pleasure. But first of all, let us consider why we want these herbs.

Parsley is used as a decoration, but it is much more than that. It is a splendid aid to the digestion of a heavy meal and a sprig with croquettes or on toasted cheese is even better eaten than admired.

Celery is equally good for purifying, turnips are a great help in getting through the winter. They must be well chewed or else they will prove indigestible (we shall be benefiting our teeth too). They contain plenty of phosphorus, which is indispensable for brain-workers, who will become especially fatigued towards the end of winter. Anyway, we were talking about greenery.

Savory is a 'must' with leguminous plants, because the latter are so difficult to digest. It is practically impossible to get savory fresh with broad beans nowadays, but we must campaign for its return, for the broad bean is a marvellous vegetable which really comes into its own when cooked with the appropriate herb.

Dill (forgotten and neglected) is more than a

pretty plant and an ingredient in pickled onions. It is also a warming herb like aniseed and cummin. Its fine green leaves will make a bland spring soup and the seeds, when infused with chamomile and perhaps valerian too, make a tea capable of bestowing a good night's rest. Dill is rich in essential oils and adds interest to plain fare. The seeds are rich in vitamin C and are a splendid addition to cheese sauce.

Thyme, which is another warming herb, eases cases of colic and attacks intestinal parasites. You know about thyme syrup for coughs; however, if you will only use the fresh thyme regularly you will have less need of the syrup. Thyme is excellent in tomato soup, with pork and, when macerated in almond oil, as drops for a minor earache.

## FAULTY EATING HABITS

If you think about herbs and what they can do for you, you will find it hard to find why they have fallen into comparative disuse. We take indigestion tablets and recommend them, as if they could do any more than relieve temporary pressure. Some cure! Does it ever occur to anyone to wonder why a stomach should be so distended? We are so far from caring that we see nothing out of the ordinary in the condition and even crack jokes about it by tapping one another on the midriff and remarking, 'I see you are doing youself well!' We should remember that every half hour someone dies of stomach cancer – 80-90 per cent mainly due to persistent faulty eating habits: always eating too much, eating too quickly, and neglecting to chew the food thoroughly, and all because there is

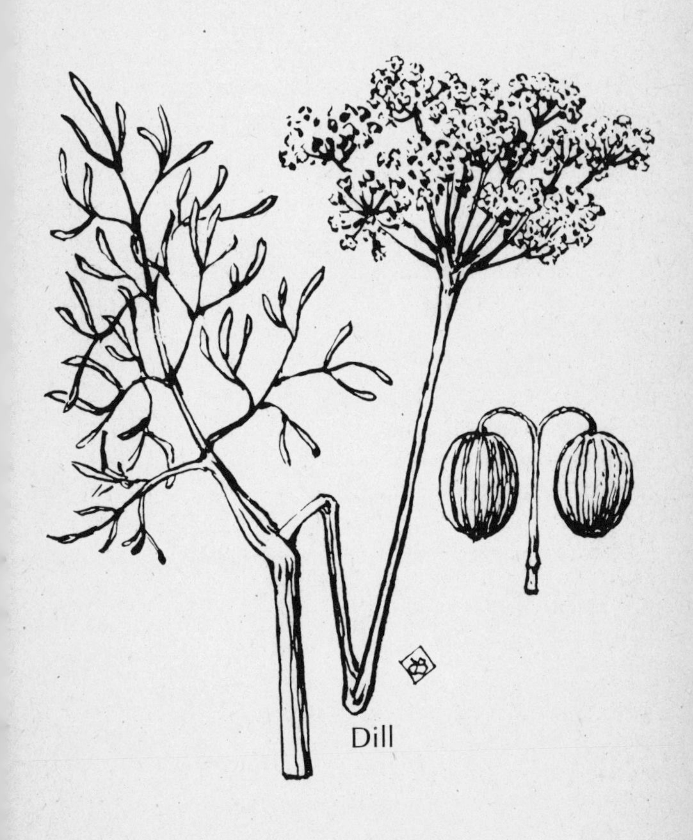

Dill

usually a lack of agreement on what is meant by good feeding.

The anaemic patient is given iron pills or liver injections by the doctor; but if he had drunk grape juice and spinach juice (squeezed out in a press) and eaten apricots he would not have had to go to the doctor in the first place.

So many diseases could be prevented if people would stop stuffing themselves with 'dainties' so injudiciously. And one can do so much with the most ordinary ingredients, which are readily available and inexpensive. Readily available did I say? Well, perhaps not invariably so at present, because ignorance has lessened the demand for them, but that need not mean that they must never become popular again – and they *will* do so if we make a determined effort to keep asking for them.

Now on to sage – who grows a sage bush in their garden nowadays? Yet it is a disinfectant and better than antibiotics because, in destroying disease germs it does not harm those bacilli which co-operate with the body and are so urgently required. These bacilli have small chance of survival in the presence of antibiotics. Fortunately, however, medical opinion is becoming more enlightened and antibiotics are being used with greater restraint.

**READY FOR THE TAKING**

Hardly anybody knows that nature has nearly all we need near by and ready for the taking. We can find it in the fields and hedgerows and are free to pick or take cuttings, as long as we do not pull off branches or dig up roots. It is amazing how everything is present in nature, and

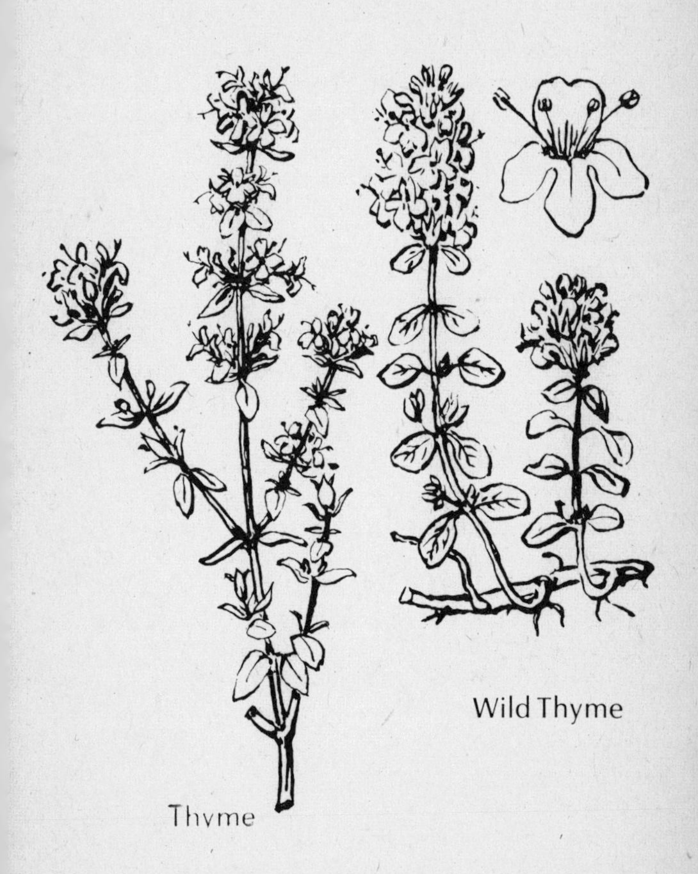
Wild Thyme
Thyme

even more amazing that we have lost sight of it. We have lost our knowledge of and trust in natural healers, preferring tablets and pills, to all those patient growing things which are standing waiting for us to come back to them.

Perhaps it it not so strange. We live in an age of concrete tower blocks, technical marvels and political upheaval. What chance have the simple things of life to engage our attention? If something is ordinary-looking we are suspicious of it. We would prefer it to be unintelligible, the brain-child of specialists, described in some mysterious technical jargon. If it is something which we ourselves can comprehend and discover we assume it must be unimportant. We look for the product of machines and test-tubes and complicated formulas, something that has the appearance of a fabulous discovery, the very incomprehensibility of which will make us bow our heads in wonder.

But we are mistaken. Other wonders beckon from humble surroundings, unnoticed by anybody, but there for all. If only people were not so impressed by formulas and technical terms, and had eyes for what lies around them!

CHAPTER SIX

# VEGETABLES NEED HERBS

If you wish to preserve your sense of well-being or vitality, your cheerfulness, good health and strength day by day, you must start with your own body and give it a fresh opportunity of following its own instincts. As I have already said, you had them as a child, but you blunted and suppressed them as you grew up. Your instincts – or what is left of them – tell you that you ought not to put up with fat, heavy and overcooked meals, but your jaded senses crave for unnatural satisfaction after a distracting day. You want to overload your stomach in order to fill the gap created by discontent and restlessness and you crush your impulses towards a finer way of life at the same time.

What is more, you suffer from stomach-ache and constipation, from fatness and headache as a direct consequence, but try to overcome them with alkaline powders, laxatives, slimming pills and aspirins. The latter may get rid of the pain but will do nothing about your distended bowels or your ill-health. Anyway, you have grown accustomed to your unhealthy condition – after all, you are no worse off in this respect than anyone else, thanks to bad feeding everywhere.

## DENATURED FOOD

Stomach powders and aspirins are constantly advertised and readily available, but sage, dill,

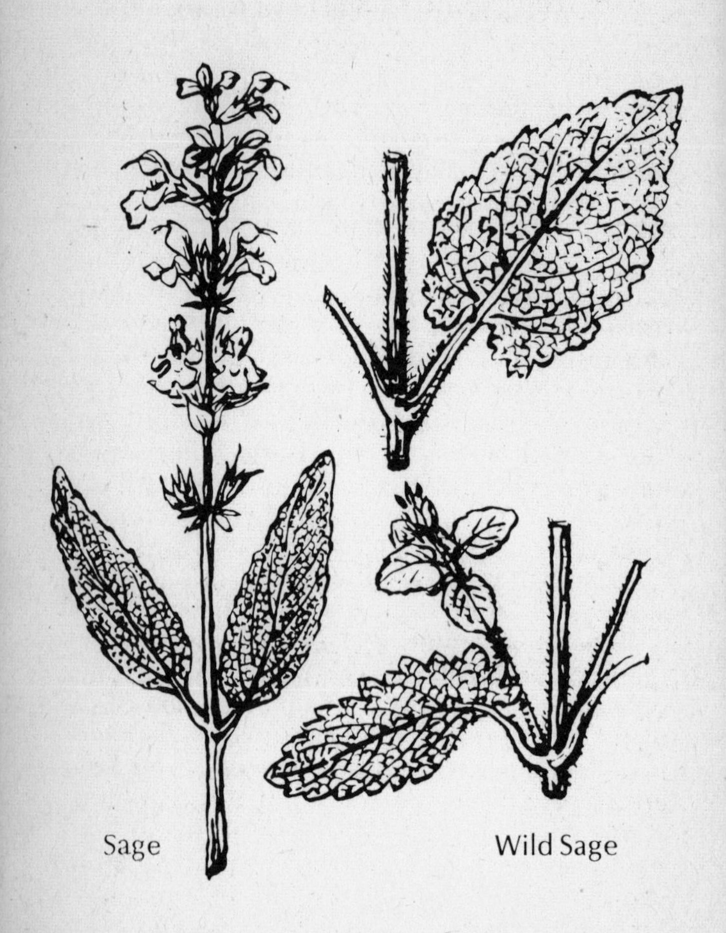
Sage
Wild Sage

thyme and the rest must be home-grown, searched for, picked or shopped round for and few know how good they are. And they *are* good: much better than chemical pills. The pharmaceutical industry can do little more than imitate nature and they market large quantities of minerals and trace elements in order to supply the deficiencies in the human organism; deficiencies which will certainly need to be made good as long as we denature our food by refining, overcooking, aerating and colouring it.

First we ruin our food for the sake of keeping it longer, making it easier to transport or more attractive looking in the stores and then pay huge sums of money for laboratory research into chemical replacements of its lost goodness. Unfortunately, chemists are unable to copy in their retorts those delicate combinations produced in living plants which are so easily assimilated by the body.

It is better to plan meals with care and judgement and include what we actually need. Let us see to it that garden produce replaces the endless stream of chemical remedies, for chemical medicaments have harmful side effects in the long run. What is more, we are only talking about 'common' vegetables which do not have to be brought from foreign climes and therefore are not expensive.

If we are now suitably impressed by the necessity for fresh vegetables and fruit and are using them daily, we should go on to add the equally essential herbs to our diet. For vegetables are not enough in themselves, they need the ancillary action of herbs to bring out the best in them. We have seen how eggs and sorrel go with spinach and savory with beans. In the same way, all fatty foods are too rich unless we put a few leaves of sage in the pan, and a dish of turnips is more tasty with rosemary.

Just try it for yourself. To begin with you will discover how marvellous it tastes, and your astonishment will turn to admiration of the harmony in nature. Soon you will find that your taste has changed drastically. Dandelions and nettles, sage, dill, thyme and marjoram are so agreeable that you will have less call for seasonings (the so-called condiments) like salt and pepper. Your sense of taste will become more refined, you will get more flavour from your food and you will become more particular about what you eat.

You will quickly come to the conclusion that prepacked potatoes, ready washed and wrapped in plastic, are not good enough and will look for the old earthy potato which is worthy of the name. You will try cooking it in the jacket too. There is no need to shudder at the thought, the flavour is marvellous.

A lot of the nutritious element of a potato is situated immediately below the skin and is removed when you peel it. Peeled potatoes must be boiled in salty water, which is then thrown away; so what is left to eat? The answer is starch, and nothing more. But bake them in their skins and open them steaming hot on the plate and discover what a potato really tastes like. Sprinkle a handful of chervil over it together with a pat of butter and eat it with salad; you will enjoy a grand meal.

The unfortunate thing about the prewashed,

prepacked supermarket products is that they are so persistently thrust under our noses, that in the end we cease to know any better. A change is called for. We must learn not only to be price conscious, but also to distinguish between what is valuable and what is valueless and to act accordingly. We must not even dream of buying an inferior article because we get more for our money. Common sense should warn us to be just as particular about what we put in our bodies as we are about what we put in our cars. We do not use inferior grades of motor oil, nor do we pump paraffin into the petrol tank for the sake of cheapness.

Well, bodies are more precious than cars and cannot be traded in for new models. So, where our bodies are concerned, we should take due care; learning to study them from all points of view and to become sensitive to the ways in which they react for good or ill. It is not so difficult to discover what suits them best and, provided we are bent on correcting our errors, there is no reason why we should be martyrs to so much pain and discomfort. You yourself will have to take the first step; you must open your eyes and observe patiently (not perfunctorily as if nothing much were wrong) and be prepared to exchange your old eating habits for better ones.

## UNDERSTAND YOUR BODY

I am not claiming that you can vanquish all ills, but I do say that you will prevent or overcome many of them. You must learn to live with and understand your body and to keep it under control, or at least to treat it as a partner in the

Marjoram

interplay of mind and body, not as an isolated unit. You should learn to regard your abdomen, hair, skin, legs and so on as a single entity, and should understand what will enable them to function as a whole.

But first you must assert your independence, making wise use of advertised products, recipes, offers and new finds if they suit you, but not being afraid to reject them if they do not fit in with your schedule. Simply follow your own road, but do abstain from half-cooked foods of convenience and those on cheap offer. I can promise you, though, that your shopping bill will not be too big. Chicory will certainly not be too dear, for it is only consumed in small quantities when raw and, if cooked in the oven, it can be eaten with a thick cheese sauce and/or an egg.

If your intake of juices, fruit, green vegetables and herbs is adequate, you can forget all the chemist's patent remedies. These will only be necessary if you dine on potatoes, meat and tinned greens day after day.

CHAPTER SEVEN

# AN INTERNAL 'SPRING CLEAN'

An independent person is one who knows that his bodily 'machine' can have different reactions from those of other people's 'machines' around him, and acts accordingly. We find it understandable that a Mini lacks the speed of a Rover. We drive them with this in mind and do not expect as much of a Mini as we do of a Rover. Why then do we make this mistake with our stomachs when we are in company? Why should we not observe our own tempo, our own likes and dislikes, without being thought of as show-offs, unsociable or even rude? The answer is that each of us is acting a part which is not our true self; we are frightened of each other's opinions, frightened to be independent and, seeking safety in numbers, shirk the responsibility for our physical welfare by conforming to what the group does.

Yes, but reliance on the group we mix with will only suffice for so long. One can avoid self-responsibility for a while and depend on others to do our thinking for us, but only for a time. This time may last twenty-five, thirty or even forty years, but finally comes the moment when we are left to fend for ourselves and then it is rather too late to stand on our own two feet, too late to come to terms with our shattered bodies, too late to do anything. Unhappily for us, this is usually the time when we are moved into an old people's home, where we are mothered and kept quiet. Never mind – we are with and under the influence of other people once again; we are all right!

## A DEMANDING SOCIETY

So you see how very much earlier you must begin to train your body and soul. This training starts with the perception of what is going on in the body. A lake is not a fen, a fountain is not a brook, and a brook is not a river, yet they are all water. In just the same way, the whole body is not 'fen', 'spring', 'brook', 'lake' or 'river' but they are all bodies. Now do not run away with the idea that I am philosophizing, even though the body does consist of more than muscles, veins, blood and glands. No I am simply talking about the body which must function day after day in a demanding society in which we are apt to lose our way somewhat. We must find the way again within our selves, and the search begins with what we so thoughtlessly 'tuck into' every day. Your feeding habits are closely related to your well-being. You will notice that, the more attention you bestow on them, the more sensitively the body responds and the better you learn what to do and what not to do. When the body learns to respond (like a well-trained horse to each knee pressure or touch of the rein) it will gradually produce finer vibrations. It would lead me too far afield to go into this, and it is not the main subject of this book; which is already idiosyncratic enough.

Nevertheless, before you are in a position to continue with your own 'training' (to pursue our horse analogy) you must bear with me a little longer. I can point out the pitfalls and traps to

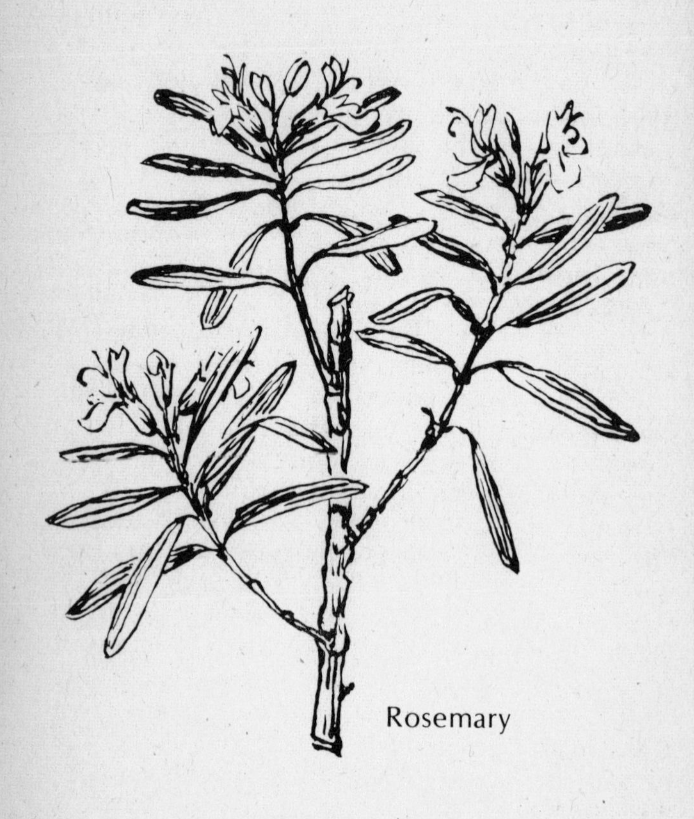

Rosemary

you because I have already surveyed the route. One thing I can guarantee: if you start in spring, you will grow slim and will beautify your skin. Begin with a regular course of stinging nettles for a month to help clear out the waste products of winter. Dandelion and plantain leaves, if added to your salads also restore vitality.

## STINGING NETTLE HAIR WASH

We can make a hair wash (also from stinging nettles) which will make the hair thick and shiny.

Boil vinegar and water (in the proportion of one part vinegar to two parts water) with a handful of nettles for 10 minutes, strain and rinse your hair with it. Wash your hair with a good herbal shampoo or with rosemary shampoo (obtainable from health food stores), and you will find out for yourself after a while. It is wonderful what this treatment will do.

If you are rather rheumatic, brew a tea of young birch leaves: take $\frac{1}{2}$ oz. (15g) leaves and just draw, do not stew them. Drink two cups per day.

Birch juice in spa water can also be taken at the end of winter for about six weeks, to give you an internal 'spring clean'.

## GARLIC FOR 'FLU

Eat plenty of garlic. Garlic is the great dilator of the blood vessels which supply the heart. It cleanses the bowels and gets rid of disease germs. Are you afraid your breath will reek of garlic? Do not give it a thought; a sprig of parsley dipped in vinegar and well chewed will kill the unpleasant smell. Just try it. If you have 'flu coming on, take a glass of warm milk and squeeze half a clove of garlic in it and see what it will do for you. However, if you find the raw plant disagreeable, take garlic capsules. Garlic is something which can be eaten all through the year, not simply in spring.

Summer is a glorious season. There are plenty of fresh fruit and vegetables about, we spend a lot of time out of doors, we swim, take walks and play sports for sheer pleasure without any urging. We devour as many good things at this time of year as would see us through the other three seasons put together. This is not always wise, as we discover to our cost in winter.

**ELDER: SOVEREIGN REMEDY**

Here is something new to add to your summer menu: elder blossom. The beautiful white umbels are a pleasure to look at, but pick a few and sprinkle a small handful into pancake batter – a forgotten treat in this country but not in France, where they still know a thing or two. Pluck up enough courage sometime to brew yourself a cup of elder flower tea, and drink it with lemon and honey. Make it exactly like ordinary tea but let it stand for six or seven minutes. It is a sovereign remedy for sore throats and tonsillitis and the taste is a revelation. It needs a little resolution to do it but anyone who does it once never regrets it.

Exactly the same may be said of lime-tree blossom. On a warm summer evening cold lime flower tea with lemon and honey is wonderfully refreshing. You should make a point of gathering the flowers when you are on holiday and

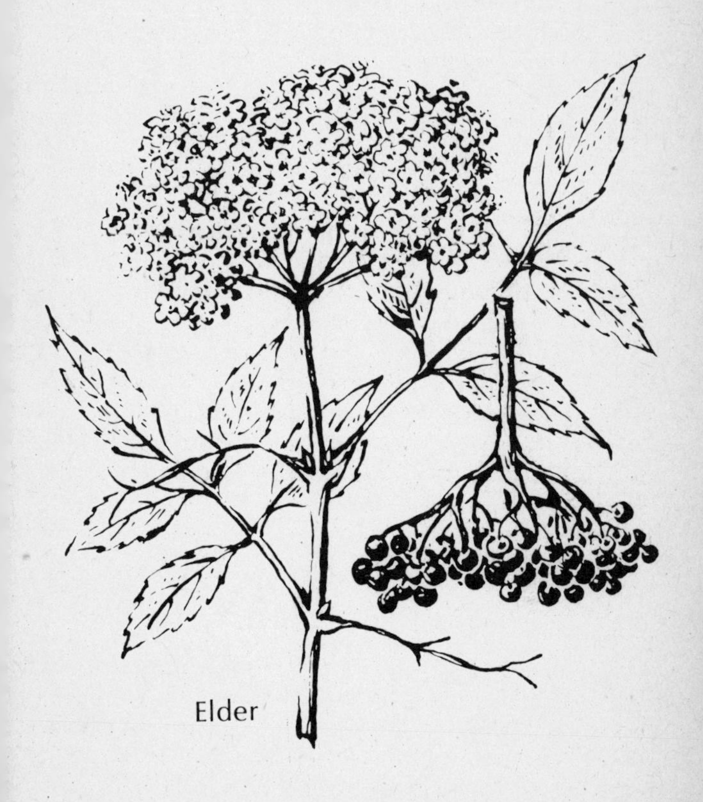
Elder

spreading them out to dry in the shade to give you a winter supply you can use for feverish colds, head colds, minor coughs and sore throats. The flowers keep well in stoppered glass jars.

Your whole summer should now be lived in the presence of natural products. Sprinkle dill and lovage and chervil into soup, eat cress and salad burnet and chervil on bread, cut up thyme, rosemary and dill with tomatoes and cucumber, and preserve a spray of dill in vinegar.

Of course you will eat plenty of tomatoes and cucumbers. Rub your skin every day with cucumber juice, which will improve it visibly. If you do the same with carrot juice or better still with the pulp which is left when you have put your carrots through the juice extractor, your skin will be rejuvenated after a short time. It will have a nice fresh colour, a good tension, and look healthy. Cucumber and carrot juice make the skin cells smooth very quickly.

# CHAPTER EIGHT

# SALADS AND JUICES

Now here are some marvellous salads. You would do yourself a good turn by trying them at least once, and once tried you will not want to do without them.

## SALAD SUGGESTIONS

**Celery Salad**
1 stick celery
2 apples
juice of ½ lemon
a pinch of sea salt
¼ pt. (150ml) sour cream
a few sunflower seeds
some grated orange peel

Scrape the celery and peel the apples and shred them. Mix with the salt, sugar, lemon juice and sour cream. Add the sunflower seeds and decorate with the orange peel.

**Carrot Salad**
2 extra large carrots
juice of ½ lemon
juice of 1 orange
1 tablespoonful honey
a few sunflower seeds *or*
some hazel-nuts
a pinch of sea salt

Grate the carrots, and add the lemon juice,

orange juice and honey. Dress with the seeds or nuts and sprinkle the salt over the top.

**Tomato Salad**

1 lb (450g) tomatoes
1 onion
a touch of basil
a little sea salt
vinegar
olive or sunflower oil

Slice the tomatoes and cover with onion rings, using the other ingredients as a salad dressing.

**Carrot and White Cabbage Salad**

1 extra large carrot
1 white cabbage
4 tablespoonsful wine vinegar
3 tablespoonsful vegetable oil
1 teaspoonful honey
1 teaspoonful mustard
some sea salt

Grate the carrot and chop the cabbage very fine. Soften the cabbage with the vinegar, then add the carrot, honey, oil and mustard. Finally, sprinkle with salt.

**Cauliflower and Banana Salad**

½ lb (225g) cauliflower
1 banana
juice of 1 lemon
1 tablespoonful currants (washed)
4 tablespoonsful cream
a little sea salt

Cut the cauliflower and banana into small

pieces and mix with the lemon juice. Whip the cream, and as soon as it is stiff scatter in the currants and carefully mix with the cauliflower and banana. Finally sprinkle with salt.

**Radish Salad**

2 bunches radishes
2 bananas
juce of ½ lemon
juice of 1 orange
a sprinkling of brown sugar
a pinch of sea salt

Mash up the bananas with a fork, mixing in the lemon and orange juice. Finely chop the radishes and pour the banana mash over. Sprinkle with a little salt and sugar.

Does this seem like hard work? Admittedly, it is harder to prepare than 'instant mash', but do not forget that the reward is far greater (as you will discover) and on top of that it will be a lot easier when this sort of meal is more familiar to you.

The most difficult part is to change your style of eating. People and their stomachs become accustomed to their eating habits, even when the latter do not agree with them as well as they should or when they put on weight. These habits belong to a pattern of behaviour and give a sense of security. You will miss (in the beginning anyway) your favourite sweets (which are no good to you), your smoked beef and ham; but if you will only persevere and take pains to prepare attractive-looking meals you will soon come to prefer them. And as soon as you are rid of your listlessness and fatigue (not to mention

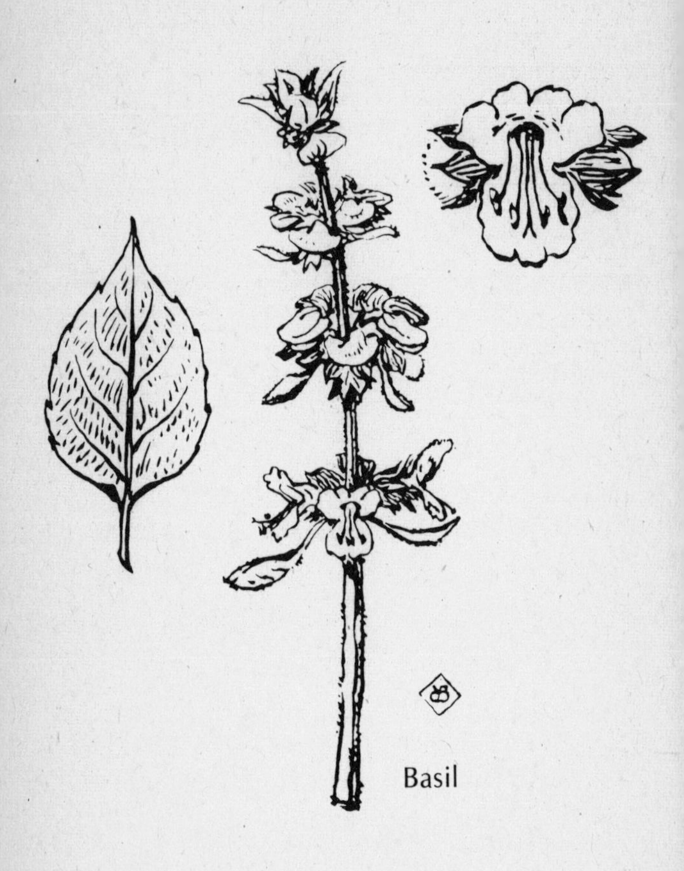

Basil

your upset stomach and heavy limbs), you will appreciate what is happening to you and then the battle will be over.

**RAW JUICE RECIPES**

You will then want to drink fresh fruit and vegetable juices instead of the usual additive-ridden bottled soft drinks.

Here are some recipes to try:

**Red Beet Juice**

$\frac{1}{2}$ beetroot juice and $\frac{1}{2}$ pineapple juice
*or*
$\frac{2}{3}$ beetroot juice and $\frac{1}{3}$ lemon juice

**Tomato Juice**

$\frac{3}{4}$ tomato juice and $\frac{1}{4}$ lemon juice with a pinch of sea salt
*or*
$\frac{1}{2}$ tomato juice and $\frac{1}{2}$ celery juice with a small slice of lemon

**Carrot Juice**

3/5 carrot juice, 1/5 celery juice and 1/5 parsley juice

**Fennel Juice**

juice of a good-sized fennel and of a grapefruit

**Strawberry Juice**

$\frac{1}{2}$ rhubarb juice and $\frac{1}{2}$ strawberry juice, a teaspoonful of honey and a small banana *puréed.*

**Pineapple Juice**

4/5 fresh pineapple juice, 1/5 cress juice and juice of a small sour apple.

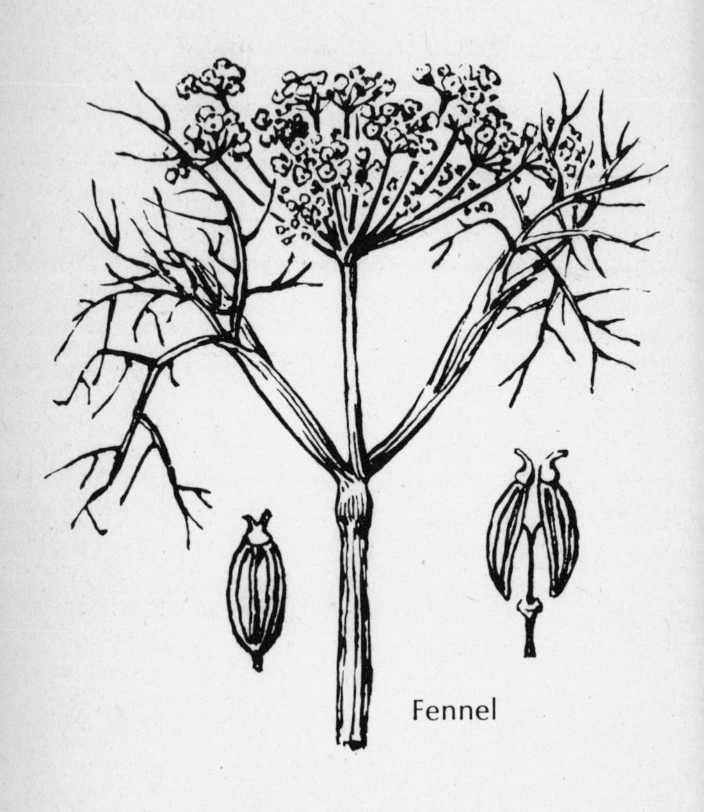
Fennel

Make it a rule to drink one of these wonderfully flavoured juices at least once a day. You will feel a lot fitter, your head will be clearer, you will find it easier to organize your time – in short, you will meet every day in a more positive fashion.

You will certainly become a good deal livelier, for melancholy and dejection are closely connected with the waste material in your body. Once this has been reduced to the normal level and you are no longer hampered by an unnecessary burden, you will become more aware and, after a while, will be able to pinpoint what is wrong when you suffer from small aches and pains. You will know, for instance, that you have been boiling your sprouts in water again and for too long and have poured the greens water down the drain and that the evil-smelling gas which is distending your bowels is your own fault. Next time you will remember and serve the sprouts with a lump of vegetable margarine, let it melt all over them and, after a quarter of an hour, they will be perfect eating.

You will also realize what the matter is when everyone is too lazy to wash up or do anything else after a meal – it usually means that the meal is too big. First a thick soup, then potatoes, meat and vegetables, followed by a semolina pudding with raisins. Well, forget the soup and replace it with half a grapefruit or a small bowl of clear soup with herbs and a slice of lemon. Do you wonder why it is so easy to find out what is wrong? It is because you immediately pay the penalty for your mistakes. You have acquired an internal barometer and you react to it directly.

CHAPTER NINE

# VARYING NEEDS

When you have got as far as this you reach the next stage. You discover where your special needs lie, and now is the time to rejoice because your body is so finely attuned that it can tell you what should and should not be put into it. Everyone is different: the 'matter-of-fact' type of person needs different food from that required by the nervy type of person. The one should have food which will lift him out of his inertia whereas the other should have as few stimulants as possible. It is important to understand and acknowledge all this. To treat every meal as an excuse for a 'good feed' regardless of its contents is a mistake. The individual who 'lives on his nerves' uses an enormous amount of energy, which he burns up during the day and has to replace at night. He ought to go for a 'constitutional' in the evening and, in general, to breathe plenty of fresh air. He should take chamomile tea, or milk flavoured with honey and aniseed, but should abstain from hot spices and should make do with as little salt as possible.

Someone else will have a constitutional tendency to become desiccated and will naturally long for cucumbers and melons, while others will find grapefruit or chicory or endives or marmalade irresistible. Let them eat what the body calls for. Yet a distinction has to be drawn between what the body really needs and the tastes it has acquired out of a sort of dissatisfaction or unhealthy craving; tastes for things like cream puffs, strong sweet coffee and so on. By this time, however, you are learning to draw such distinctions for yourself.

The better you learn to sense correctly what you need, the less you will want quick snacks like chocolates and cakes between meals. The children will not bother about sweets so much either and, when they do, they can be given nuts or raisins as in the old days.

The more balanced your diet is the less you will turn to something to 'tide you over' between meals; in any case, do not keep your stomach 'topped up' during the day, it benefits from order and regularity. It must have periods of rest.

## EDIBLE FLOWERS

If you have kept pace with me so far, how about going a step further? You have learnt the value of stinging nettles, dandelions, sorrel, cress and Swiss-style muesli. You have become accustomed to these unusual eatables. Very well, now let us go outside again, this time to pick and eat the daisies. Everyone knows them but nobody eats them, although it is perfectly possible to do so. A few of the flower heads scattered on top of the salad will make it look most attractive and are helpful for de-acidifying the blood too.

Or, prepare a salad of nasturtium flowers with a dressing of olive oil, lemon juice and sugar. A little orange-coloured salad like this is marvellous – a treat fit for a king. Blue borage flowers are also very tasty, just like the cornflower blooms used to decorate a salad dish.

Nasturtium

Flowers contain the finest ethereal oils, which can keep the body young and resilient. The violet and the glittering acacia are also edible. But do not eat them thoughtlessly; they are not meant to be bolted, nor eaten as if it were all a 'bit of a joke'.

Try to feel some of the wonder and respect due to something marvellous. By which I mean, never eat a flower with one quick bite and a swallow. Nature's finest products should be transmuted within you, as it were, transforming you into another person in many ways. I say this quite literally, for it is unthinkable that, after some months of such a light diet, you will want to go back to the old, heavy menu, especially as you begin to recognize what is happening inside you and to know what is good and what is bad for you, what you ought and what you ought not to do.

## A MIND OF YOUR OWN

A great deal of the misery in the world stems from the fact that people do not know their own best course of action. They allow themselves to be pushed around and manipulated by scientists and politicians because they are incapable of forming their own opinions, and follow the man who has the smoothest line of patter.

This is how people can be constantly misled. Each should choose his or her own way of life. We have minds of our own to make up and should express our own thoughts and be prepared to take a firm stand on what we think is and is not important. It may sound odd, but your nourishment is closely involved here.

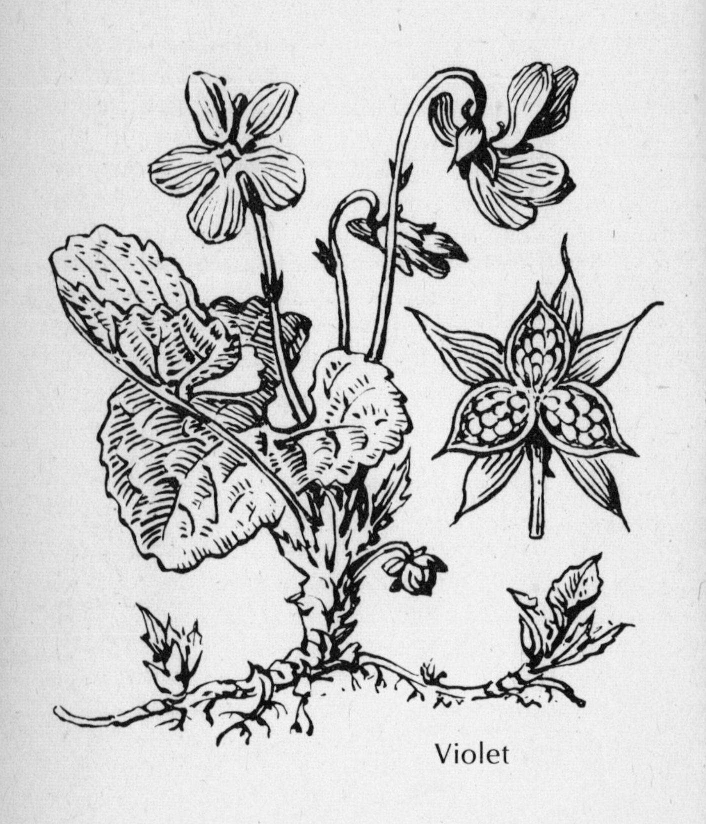

Violet

Once your insides have been cleansed a little, your digestive tract, which is the seat of the emotions, will become purer and you will be able to tell when an emotion is really your own and when it is mere sentimentality or keeping in step with the rest of the crowd.

Perhaps you will dismiss what I have just said with a shrug of the shoulders, but I assure you it is perfectly true. You have only to put it to the test. A person who is 'clean inside' has a clearer picture of the outside world, and one full of vitality is in a better position to ignore cajolery and rely on his own judgment. In a spineless society everything depends on individuals who refuse to be trifled with. The people themselves must wake up and make their approval and disapproval heard and then act on it too; not by mass demonstrations and organized protests but by refusing to be persuaded out of what they think is best.

We can strike our first blow for independence by avoiding all the things which are represented as being healthgiving and delicious and good but are nothing of the sort. Generally speaking, there is nothing wholesome about processed, heat-treated, coloured, preserved, refined or flavoured foods. They are quick to serve certainly, but natural foods can be prepared just as quickly and are ever so much better.

CHAPTER TEN

# JAMS, JELLIES, SAUCES AND SOUPS

As a rough estimate, you can make do with one-third of your usual food intake. So, when you change to dearer produce like plant oil, fresh vegetables and raw juices, your cash outlay is no greater because you are having to buy less and, as you will be providing a lot of things for yourself anyway, you can stop worrying about health food shops being more expensive.

**Elderberry Syrup**
Place the berries in a pan with sufficient water to cover the bottom, and boil thoroughly. Strain, sieve and make up to 2 pt. (1 litre). Add 1½ lb (750g) sugar and bring back to the boil. Store in sterilized bottles and drink for feverish and heavy colds.

Make some elderberry and rowan berry (mountain ash) jam too. Let the rowan berries steep overnight in one part vinegar and two parts water. Strain the next day and boil in a small quantity of water. It is a distinctive, bitter jam, exclusively for connoisseurs.

**Tomato Sauce**
5 lb (2½kg) ripe tomatoes
½ pt. (¼l) wine vinegar
2 onions
2 cloves of garlic
10 peppercorns

2 bay leaves
3 cloves
as much ginger as will go on the point of a knife
a little mustard

Warm the tomatoes and pass them through a sieve. Mix the chopped onions and garlic, the spices and the wine vinegar with the tomato *purée* and cook for quarter of an hour. Pass again through a fine sieve and cook for 5 more minutes. The sauce must have the consistency of cream; if not, boil until it does. A little brown sugar may be added to taste. Pour into sterilized bottles while still hot and seal well. *It will keep indefinitely.*

This sauce can be used for soups, with meat, as a drink and as an additive to cheese sauce for leeks. Once you have made it, you will want to have it in store every winter, but then the same is true of elderberry and rowan berry jam.

**Tomato Jam**
2 lb (1kg) small green tomatoes
1½ lb (750g) sugar
½ lemon

Wash and dry the tomatoes cut them into thin slices and allow to stand in the sugar for 24 hours. Put the mixture in the saucepan together with very thin slices of lemon (without pips). Bring to the boil slowly, stirring occasionally. The jam is ready when it has turned an amber colour.

Tomatoes are very cheap at certain times of the year. Here, then, are a few special recipes so that you can make the best use of them when they are plentiful:

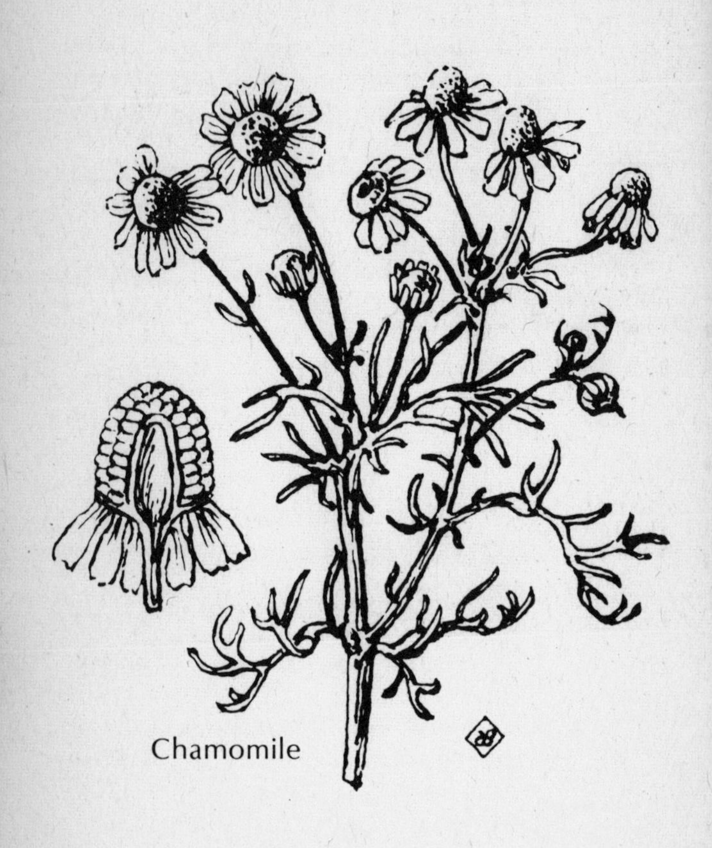

Chamomile

**Green Tomatoes with Meat**
Boil the tomatoes in water, peel them, chop up fine and mix with a finely chopped onion, salt, pepper and oil. Allow to stand for a few hours and serve with beef.

**Green Tomato Sauce**
Cut up a garlic bulb into slices and fry in oil until brown. Add finely chopped sage and a few ladlesful of clear soup. Put the sliced tomatoes into this sauce with a little salt and pepper. To thicken beat an egg yolk and add.

**Tomato Preserve**
Rub the skins off whole ripe tomatoes and put in a jar with dill and, if desired, other kitchen herbs. Add spiced vinegar which has been boiled and left to cool and allow to stand.

**Tomato Jelly**
Chop up some ripe tomatoes and cook until soft in their own juice. Sieve and boil the pulp. Sieve again, then spread out on plates and allow to dry in the oven. You will now have a leathery pulp which can be kept very dry in jars or tins. When required, dissolve a piece in warm water and use for sauces, soups and so on.

*This will keep for several years*

Here is another special recipe. This time for quince.

**Quince Jelly**
2 lb (1kg) quinces
4½ pt. (2l) water
2 lb (1kg) sugar

Wash the quince fruit, dry and rub clean. Cut up the fruit into sections, remove the cores and tie them inside a cloth. Place the quince sections and the bag of cores in a pan with the water and boil until the fruit is really soft. Pass the fruit through a sieve by allowing it to seep through for several hours without pressing or stirring. Weigh out 2 lb (1kg) sugar for every 2 pt. (1 litre) juice. Add and bring mixture to the boil and simmer until the last drop to fall from the skimmer is nice and round. Then put into jars.

It is amazing how many wonderful things are ready to hand in nature. It is equally amazing how little use is made of them. They seem to have been forgotten in this age of semi-processed and fully-processed foods; but neither the factory nor the laboratory can offer what nature supplies. The most exquisite aromas and the highest food values are to be found in plants which have been permitted to grow without human interference, that is to say, without artificial fertilizers, growth-promoting additives or insecticides. The sun and the rain give them what they need if they are left alone, but wild plants shrink from meddling. The folk who dwell beyond the borders of nature's empire have almost forgotten what real chamomile and plantain look like. They must venture into the country again if they are going to rediscover them.

## CELERY

Celery, for example, is available everywhere at all seasons and is never too expensive. It contains vitamins A, B and C and is full of the

Plantain

phosphorus which is so essential for growing school children and, in general, for people who have plenty of brainwork to do. Those whose intake of phosphorus is too low become forgetful. Eat the celery raw, as a salad with nuts and raisins, or eat it in soup.

**CELERY SOUP**

Cook a large stick of celery in clear soup and pass it through a sieve, adding a dash of cream and a sprinkling of grated cheese as the final touch.

**SPINACH**

Here is another indispensable vegetable and it is still on sale fresh, although I fear we shall lose this privilege fairly soon if the warning is not sounded. Spinach is very perishable and a problem for the greengrocer. You will shortly find that shopkeepers will be saying that tinned or deep-frozen spinach is just as good and much more convenient. The second statement is true but the first is decidedly false. Refuse to be put off with tinned or frozen spinach and persist in asking for the fresh form.

The will of the majority must prevail if we make it felt. 'There's no demand for it' is the familiar answer to the question why a product is no longer being sold. Let us ensure that it will not work as far as fresh vegetables are concerned. Spinach stimulates the formation of the red blood cells and purifies the intestines. Spinach soup, when it first comes in early in the season is a real 'pick-me-up' in spring. Heat up some vegetable soup and throw in a good handful of finely chopped spinach at the last moment, sprinkle with grated cheese and serve with *croûtons.*

Cabbage and lettuce salad is deservedly popular. Eaten at the beginning of a meal, it gets the digestive juices working. If you are suffering from obstinate acne, (which is nothing more than intestinal poisons which have found themselves an outlet via the skin), wash the affected parts in cabbage water.

Leeks have vitamins B and C and contain sulphuric acid which carries off water and is a genuine remedy for rheumatic sufferers. Endive and chicory are bitter vegetables which stimulate the heart and liver. A salad of chicory and endives will do you a great deal of good when taken at the beginning of meals in winter.

## CHICORY SALAD

Cut up 2 or 3 stumps of chicory very fine and mix with sunflower oil and a drop of lemon juice. Stir in some raisins and a grated apple together with a handful of sunflower seeds.

## BEETROOT COCKTAILS

Young beetroot are always suitable to eat raw or squeezed for the juice. Beets contain a lot of natural sugar and are an important source of energy. In young beets you can also squeeze the stalks and leaves.

1. 4 oz. (100g) apple juice
   2 oz. (50g) carrot juice
   1 oz. (25g) beetroot juice

2. 5 oz. (150g) apple juice
   2 oz. (50g) beetroot juice
   2 oz. (50g) lemon juice

3. 4 oz. (100g) apple juice
   2 oz. (50g) beetroot juice
   2 oz. (50g) orange juice

4. 1 oz. (25g) sauerkraut juice
   1 oz. (25g) beetroot juice
   4 oz. (100g) apple juice
   1 oz. (25g) tomato juice

If you do not possess a centrifugal juice extractor it is a pity. Infants, the elderly, young mothers, invalids and those who are overworked definitely need one or other of the fruit or vegetable juices every day.

You will get years of pleasure from a juicer, and when I say years I am thinking of all the daily use these years represent. An extractor like this is indispensable to the older citizen who wants to prolong his or her useful life. All sorts of small ailments which are potentially serious can be dealt with early if caught in time and treated properly. A juice can prove particularly helpful with people who stubbornly cling to their old eating habits. Practically everyone likes fruit juice and mixing the juices with vegetables is not such a big break with tradition. There is no need for anaemia, high and low blood-pressure, intestinal disorders, headaches or stomachaches. There is no need for pep pills and potions. Most of our ailments would not occur if we knew more about the whys and wherefores of what we were eating.

CHAPTER ELEVEN

# NUTRITION IS A SCIENCE

Children ought to be taught just as much about healthy feeding as about reading, writing and arithmetic. It is incomprehensible (and reprehensible too) that so far most schools have overlooked this aspect of education. Instruction in the fundamentals of diet should not be confined to the domestic science colleges but should be given in the ordinary schools. Young people should be shown how to feed sensibly in order to fit themselves for adult life; just as they learn how to write a letter, read a book and calculate for the same reason. Eating is something they will do every day and that is precisely why it is so important.

The anaemic must no longer resort to iron tablets. Our hospitals are too full; the doctors are overworked, and 80 per cent of their patients consult them for chronic fatigue, headache and feverish colds. This 80 per cent must learn to help themselves and to call in the doctor only when he is really needed; the responsibility rests with the individual. Lessons at school on wise feeding would aid them in exercising this responsibility. We all sit down to three square meals a day, but dismiss the A B C of correct feeding as unimportant. The criterion for most persons is, 'I enjoy that' or, 'I don't think much of that', and these judgements depend on their family habits and upbringing.

Ignorance and laziness are the culprits which

fly in the face of the first signs of trouble. Feeding and the knowledge of nutrition is a science which deserves to be taught. It has nothing to do with what is easy or quick to prepare, but with what the body needs day by day and why. Ease and quickness are not important, although I hasten to add that they need not be sacrificed if you know what you are doing. Muesli is no more work to prepare than the average breakfast if you set about it the right way and arrange the apple, lemon, nuts, honey and cream beside the bowl of oat flakes. Uncooked foods are not complicated.

You must acquire insight and good organization, the rest is no more demanding than the old type of cooking.

## HEALTH FOODS PRODUCE CLEAR COMPLEXIONS

Meals, we are told, must always be appetizing, because, 'one deserves it after a hard day's work'. Let that be as it may; even though meals should be appetizing, health, vitality, a clear head, the ability to concentrate, all come before tastiness, and all these benefits must come from your food, not from the chemist's. What is more, even your clear complexion is produced by what you eat and not by the pots of chemically manufactured face creams.

It is marvellous what is available to you, and how inexpensive it is. There are impressive and highly priced cosmetics in the shops, but do you realize that you can make three-quarters at least of what you need?

Cucumbers, tomatoes, chamomile, olive oil, apricot *purée* and carrot pulp are a few ex-

Borage

amples only from a whole range of materials. You make a mask of yogurt or sour cream, of curds or of an egg yolk with fruit pulp and a drop of lemon juice well stirred in. You will discover what suits you best after two or three trials and the results will astonish you. Tone up your neck with a mask of bran and lemon, and rub a generous amount of carrot *purée* into your whole skin after a bath or shower.

We must get back to nature and take an interest in what she has to offer and regain our respect for what grows and lives around us. Then we shall appreciate what nature means and shall be able to enter with more right and enthusiasm into the battle *for* conservation and *against* crop-spraying, *for* planning and *against* pollution, *for* natural foodstuffs and *against* denaturing, *for* pure water and *against* fluoridation; for then we know just where we are. We must reject poisons and colouring matter, essences and bleaching agents, and irradiated and sprayed foodstuffs which are 'improved' in an endless variety of ways at the cost of their intrinsic goodness. The consumers themselves must take issue with what is being 'forced down their throats'. Those who do not wish to eat rubbish, must not buy rubbish; but this requires a knowledge of what they are doing in the first place.

**BATTERY HENS**

Let us think of eggs for a minute. I dare say you buy 'farm-fresh' eggs? Well, have you ever seen battery hens? Nothing could be further removed from what is proper to living creatures. If possible the industry would have the hens laying at regular intervals on to conveyor belts. The hens are treated like machines even as it is. They are wedged into individual compartments behind a feeding trough, and the light is turned on day and night.

After a year the hens are worn out and old, but no one cares; a new generation has meanwhile been hatched in the incubator and is ready to take the place of the one that has been 'exhausted'. They lay twice as many eggs as the free-range hens, but they lay eggs which have half the food value and a third of the taste. However, who worries about that? But then have you ever eaten new-laid eggs from free-range poultry?

Tests have already been made to get shell-less eggs, packed in a sort of plastic bag. These things are still called 'eggs' of course, and if they are held under the noses of shoppers for long enough nobody will know any better. Nice and easy to transport and very economical. Economy above all else. Have people gone mad? It looks like it.

There is a similar state of affairs in pork production. The order of the day is 'Breed, breed, breed – earn, earn, earn'. Everything is going splendidly, except for the living conditions and the health of the animals – until we discover that the abused and caged creatures are no longer able to stand on their trotters. No matter, we slaughter them before they have the chance to fall down and then we have meat of 'high' quality ... Some hope! We rear our calves in dark boxes for the sake of white veal, but most of us do not enquire too closely into this and so we avoid any feeling of shame; besides it makes money.

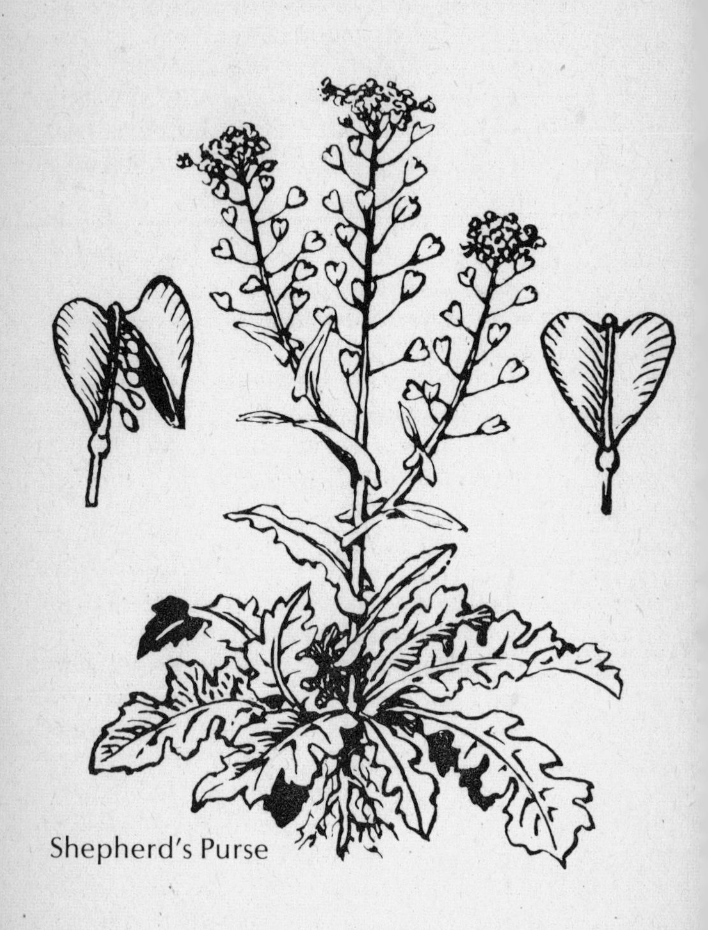

Shepherd's Purse

What action can be taken by each one of us personally? Well, if we will eat meat, let us make sure that the animal from which it comes was well treated. Let us ensure that it is not the sort of meat which ought to stick in our throats. We may feel that we should only be making fools of ourselves by being so fussy, but we are responsible people, and the onus is on us to find out what is happening for ourselves. My opinion is that it is not something being done for the benefit of you and your health, it is not a search for improved flavour, it is a frantic struggle for money.

**A WEAKER GENERATION**

Industry is insane, the economy is insane and the consumers are insane. Everything must show a profit and with this in mind we spray, denature, can and colour our food and, as far as possible, make synthetic imitations of the genuine article. If at all feasible, the natural product is replaced by the chemical one in the hope that the former will gradually be forgotten by the public. Hardly has this happened than we discover that the natural product contains a 'little something' that is missing from its chemical copy. That 'little something' is irreplaceable in fact. In the meantime a weaker generation has grown up, with hair that falls out earlier, teeth which decay earlier and a catastrophic history of cardiac and circulatory disorders.

People are beginning to fall victims to the fate they have meted out to the animals. They too are herded into cramped living quarters and pushed so close together that they have to be prevented from attacking one another out of sheer nervous frustration. They are fed with fried potatoes, hamburgers and white bread and try to keep going on aspirins and stomach pills.

How often have you heard someone say 'I don't know where I would be without aspirins!'? Things have reached such a pass that reliance on the latter has become a commonplace. 'What the eye doesn't see, the heart won't grieve for', our mothers used to tell us, but that is no longer good enough where foodstuffs are concerned, as a visit to your nearest hospital or doctor's waiting room will show. It is your shattered health you have to grieve for.

This general ignorance will prevail as long as rational instruction on nutrition is missing from our school timetables. As I have already pointed out, when we know what we are doing we shall no more dream of putting the wrong fuel in our bodies than we do in our cars. The day will come when we shall set store by an existence worthy of humanity, and then we shall build towns where everyone has their own allotment to cultivate; not urban deserts with an afterthought of parks where we are warned to 'keep off the grass'.

'Not a very economical proposal' you say? Maybe not, but we are talking about human beings and their food, not about machines which can be conveniently and completely stowed away. I assume, of course, that we want the human beings of the future to retain their humanity.

## SELF-AWARENESS AND HEALTH

So far I have been talking to you about getting well and keeping well. Here, and in the final chapter, I hope to review the 'common' illnesses and indispositions, and to look at what we can do about them without having to fall back on what the pharmaceutical industry has to offer. The latter will not rid us of the diseases, but merely relieve the symptoms.

Please do not run away with the idea that I am trying to do the doctors out of a job. What I intend doing is to discuss the ordinary sicknesses and infirmities which you and I encounter, for which we often hold the remedy in our own hands. Generally speaking, we are well able to help ourselves where minor complaints are concerned and, if we do not neglect small ailments or ignore warnings, we can largely prevent the more serious maladies.

## POISONED BOWELS ENCOURAGE DISEASE

Toxic intestines are the major source of misery. You can take my word for it that they encourage all diseases. Our bowels are in a poisonous condition nearly all the time; a condition which is our own fault. We ignore sound advice on diet, we eat what we like and as much as we like and, when we have finally finished the sweet course, we have not the slightest idea as to whether or not what we have just had is truly nourishing or properly prepared.

Now by proper preparation I mean the way the food is grown as much as anything. And how that is bungled! It is just too silly! We allow ourselves to be so overruled by the food industry that we blindly imagine that what suits the manufacturers is good for us too. Do not be deceived. They set out with good intentions no doubt, but seem to get trapped in a gigantic game of 'beggar my neighbour' as far as other manufacturers are concerned. Each wants a bigger and better factory. It is unbelievable what injurious rubbish we buy. And what is even more incredible is that we have grown so used to it that we think it is fine and good for us. However, the day will dawn when lots of things will be too dear to buy, so it makes sense for us to learn to look after ourselves.

**MORE ABOUT CHEWING**

We were talking about bowel impurities, and it is here that everything starts to go wrong; this is where our troubles begin. Our headaches, pimples, ulcers and inflammations can be traced back to them. So what can we do? We can chew! We can take up chewing in deadly earnest. Let us start a chewing craze – a national chewing campaign, with banners down the street, leaflets, TV programmes, chewing lessons in school and chewing games.

Let me give you an example. Take a piece of bread in your mouth and chew it. It is ten to one that you will swallow it before it is hardly tasted. In other words, you have not chewed it properly. Your attention was diverted too quickly and you swallowed pieces which were too big. The same is true of everything you eat. You eat while you are on the phone, or reading the paper, or talking or complaining or drinking. And what happens? Your intestines are overloaded with the lumpy morsels and cannot get rid of them, and then begins the fermentation, the acid production, the stoppage, the hardening, the torpidity, the compaction, and so on.

Chewing is the kingpin of our digestive processes, in which we can take no further active part once the food has passed our gullets. There you have the source of nearly all our diseases.

'Why, it's so easy!', some of you will exclaim. Easy, yes, but difficult all the same to some. Try it for yourself.

You will make another discovery, too. Not only do you chew carelessly, you do almost everything carelessly: telephoning, laying the table, dressing, walking around – you name it. You go for a walk say, or lay the table, or entertain company, but your mind is elsewhere. It is immensely difficult to keep your mind on what you are doing the whole time, and to be actively conscious that you are doing what you are doing, whether it is telephoning, laying the table, walking, entertaining, or the like.

'How do *you* know?', you may ask, and I shall reply, 'Why not find out for yourself?' For instance, start to lay a table with the idea of thinking about nothing else. Half-way through, your resolution will have been forgotten. It is so curious how we are locked up inside ourselves; how we do or refrain from doing, act or react, like programmed puppets. As soon as we break the vicious circle and start acting for ourselves, no end of difficulties can be resolved. For we are not living *life* up; living is using *us* up. We make our own selves ill.

## GLANDULAR SECRETIONS

When we are moody, touchy, or cynical, our

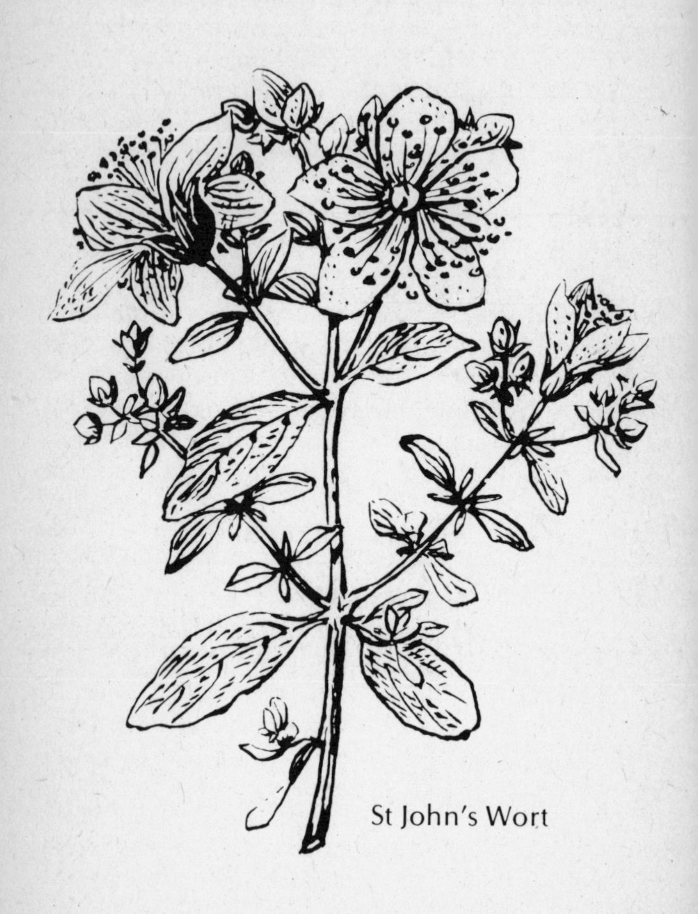

St John's Wort

glands secrete substances which influence us adversely: harsh chemicals which chafe, gnaw or rasp and, in the end, injure certain organs, whichever are the weakest (the weakest link in the chain, as we term it). The same applies to jealousy, fear, suspicion, anger and the like. We also secrete chemicals when experiencing feelings of joy, love, friendship and cheerfulness; chemicals which are compatible with us and will benefit our bodily processes. It is striking how many opportunities we have to mould our own destinies and equally striking how little we know how to seize them.

We bob about like a cork at sea, tossed to and fro by the waves – the waves of public opinion, current ideas and fashion. If only we had our own opinions and ideas, we should not become so physically upset by it all. We should not be getting headaches from rage, stomachaches from annoyance or griping from a sense of impotence. But then to do this we must try to find ourselves. We must ask ourselves questions like, 'What do I think, what do I know, what do I want, what will I permit?' Whoever can answer these questions truthfully, will find himself and learn to help himself.

## BECOMING AWARE

It is a process of simply becoming aware, although in one sense of the word there is nothing simple about it. You learn to recognize what you are doing each moment of the day. At first, you will find it impossible; but persevere. Learn the feel of your hand as it writes, the contraction of the fingers, the tension in the forearm, the stiffness in the neck muscles. Feel them and discover how much more relaxed they could be.

You will note that your neck muscles tighten up too often during the day (when you are self-conscious, when you are aggressive, when you are pushing yourself too hard to when you are engaged in a difficult phone call) and that this tightening of the neck muscles induces headaches – headaches for which relaxation, not aspirin, is the remedy. It is important to realize how thoroughly your neck has tensed up. However, this sort of realization only comes to the person who studies himself a great deal. Is that egotistical? Call it so if you like, but become an 'egotist' as you name it, even so, because that is the only way to be helped. You must help yourself.

The individual who does not learn to know himself will certainly fail to understand others except in terms of worthless 'current opinion' which feeds on sentiment. He will follow the trend; saying, for instance, that American intervention in Vietnam was 'good' and Cuban intervention in Angola 'bad' or vice versa, according to the accepted view in his particular circle.

## DEEP BREATHING

When you do your 'daily dozen' in the morning, take three deep breaths in the bedroom and exhale even more deeply if possible. Obliterate every thought except that of your respiration. You will notice straight away that your breathing has gained something extra for the rest of the day. It is a vitally important function. It activates your diaphragm and your abdominal organs, your circulation and your heart muscles. Your 'body stove' is blown to a blaze in every corner so to speak. Dead places (places where colds start) come to life and regain their functions after a while. You have only to try it to see that I am right; but do continue for several days before passing judgement.

Phone, write, knit, walk, run, talk or work, and live each moment of the activity in the vivid realization of what you are doing. It is a striking sensation if you succeed, but it will probably be very fleeting. The rest of the time you will be a reservoir of uncontrolled and disorganized actions.

Your body reacts to everything you do in much the same way as a seismograph reacts to an earthquake, and is shaken this way and that by your emotions, with unfavourable consequences for your health. Then, when you are ill, specialized treatment is available to make you better.

All the same, specialized medical treatment has no knowledge of what you are in yourself. It can only tackle the symptoms with more or less result. Yet there is always the possibility of a relapse; because it is your symptoms, not you yourself, which have been treated. Your symptoms have been given prominence, isolated and 'put on the operating table' so to speak, but you have not been treated as an undivided whole. Consequently you return to the point of origin of the complaint and 'step on board' the selfsame 'roundabout' of disease creation. Nevertheless, this need not happen. There are a number of things you can do.

First there is your daily food. Know what, why

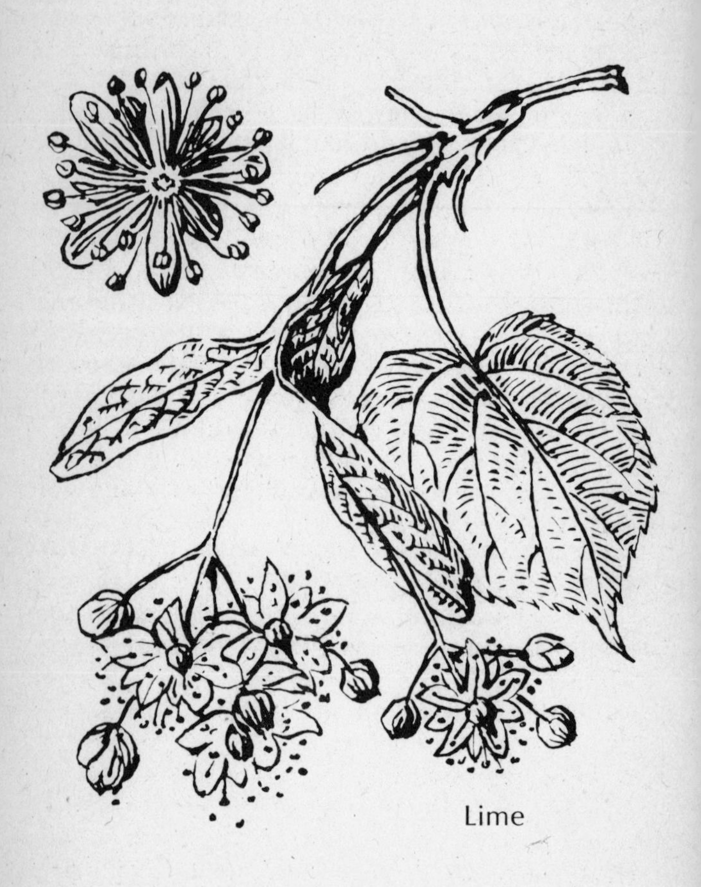

Lime

and when you eat. Keep your blood and intestines clean by eating suitably. Foods do exist that will help in this, and they are readily available in nature. Not much longer, however, for we are exterminating them as fast as we can out of sheer ignorance, and the situation will only be altered when literally everybody realizes what is going on and takes positive action.

For instance, it is not true that you can do nothing with onions because they give you 'wind'. Leeks and cabbage need not disagree with you either. They lie 'heavy on the stomach' simply because one of your organs is already out of order. They indicate that you are already unwell. When you are well, they will not trouble you. But you eat too much, you overcook the food, you pour the goodness down the sink, you do not chew, and you eat the wrong things. It never crosses your mind that you are putting too much inside you, or cooking too long. You do not give thought to *what* you are eating. All you do is eat.

Perhaps you are annoyed at my being so abrupt and pointed. I am in the right though. Your body is like a taxi and you are like the driver. You accept any 'fare' that hails you! The difference is that you are not paid. You are the one who pays, for everything that enters your body leaves a trace. If you will only identify these traces by paying close attention you will know exactly what should and what should not be given admittance.

The next thing – which everyone can do – is to observe what happens to oneself. This is a very painful process, for one discovers that a lot goes on with which one is not in agreement. You race backwards and forwards unnecessarily, or else you sit about too much; you are too lazy or needlessly active; you have to be part of a crowd or you like keeping yourself to yourself more than you should; you are too ready to sympathize with others or easily become angry with them; you assert yourself or you hide your light under a bushel.

## HEIGHTENED SELF-CONSCIOUSNESS

These are facts of which you are generally unaware. You do notice them occasionally but not at the moment they occur. You scribble inattentively, you drink your tea inattentively, you chew inattentively and you chat inattentively. In doing so, you involve your body chemistry without thought and you are affected in ways in which you ought not to be affected. You would not be so affected if you put yourself into whatever you do. When you spit, spit. When you think, think. When you eat, eat. When you pass water, pass water. We use but a third of our lungs and a fifth of our brain capacity. All this must be exploited, but it will continue to lie fallow unless you concentrate on what you are doing or heighten your consciousness. I do not mean being conscious of what is going on around us, but conscious of what is happening with us, through us, in us and to us.

So first we shall learn how to operate our own switchboards: to get the blood pumping through our bodies, to remove the waste material, to expel poisons, to resuscitate dead places, to bring inactive centres back into play. In short, to take charge of our lives. A lot is involved and it is quite an enterprise, but the person stakes are high.

Now, I do not want you to run away with the idea that I am an expert. I am like a musician who has just left the conservatory, with lots of learning and little experience. However, my experience to date is so amazing that it would be a sin and a shame to keep it to myself. Believe me, we can do so much more with our bodies than we think possible. They can get well of their own accord. Yet we bungle everything so dreadfully that we take it for granted that all that can be done is to patch them up. Now, anyone who treats his body with some insight, will find no need to patch it up; there will be nothing damaged to repair.

Surely, if the present trend continues, society is quite likely to collapse altogether. We are being stifled with 'do's' and 'don'ts', crushed in the race for material prosperity and carried away by the absurd glorification of technology and science and by the equally absurd rejections of emotionalism and expressiveness.

We are very gratified if our children are impractical but brainy, and only moderately pleased with the reverse situation. We see brains in terms of pounds and manual skill in terms of pence. Such an attitude is a recipe for social decay, and so are the rules we have created. We count success by what we earn, where we live, what sort of job we do, and not by personal happiness.

The new generation have been trying to wriggle out of this strait-jacket, but it is laced too tightly for them. That is because we are not living from inside to outside but from outside to

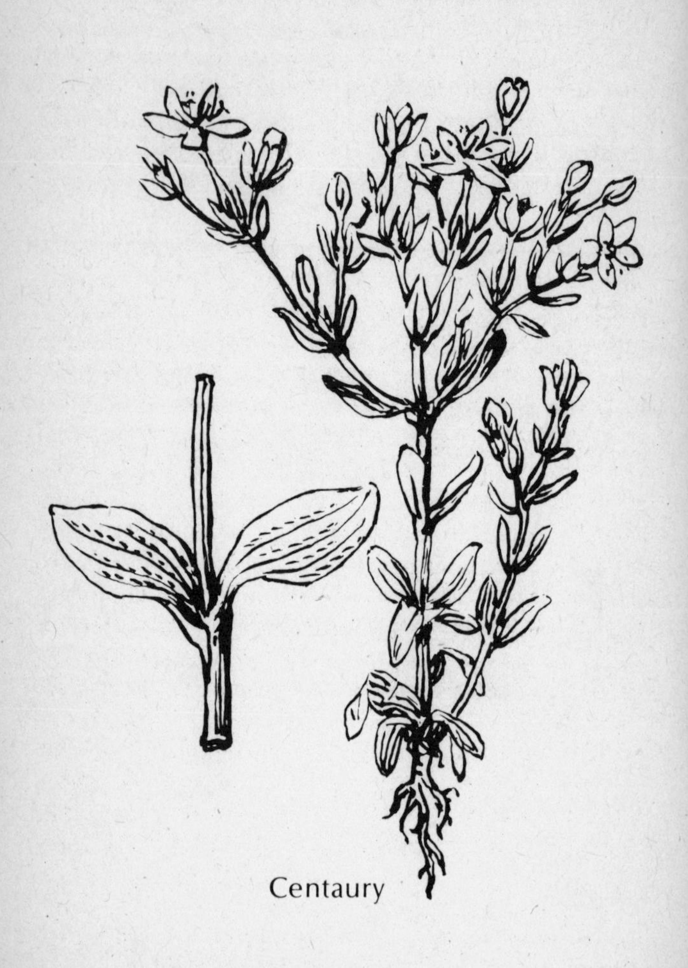

Centaury

inside. If we do not assert our own identities and ignore what 'people say', we shall never escape from the mad merry-go-round of present-day life.

If you want to change the world, begin with yourself. An over-worked cliché, yes, but how true! Begin wildly, however, and you will accomplish nothing. You must begin at the beginning; organized and controlled by yourself.

## THE TRULY WISE

Once you have mastered your body, your soul (and this is a concept we cannot discuss here) will take notice of that clean body. It will transmit signals to which you were formerly deaf. But then we must shut our eyes and ears to soulless slogans, rules, restrictions and regulations, and from the world too as it is today. It is high time we said, 'thus far and no farther'. The claptrap of the politicians, the establishment scientists, the technologists, and the sociologists and economists must be silenced. We must join forces with the truly wise; with people who are not striving for honours, position, votes, power or titles, who are not feathering their nests or working for the membership of their group or union or sub-limating some personal 'hang-up' in the guise of a public-spirited campaign. Let us co-operate with those who know and understand.

There are such people in the world but they do not raise their voices like fairground hucksters. They work behind the scenes, burrowing below the surface as it were, but the stones they throw up are starting to make big, spreading ripples in the public 'duck-pond'. Each of us can work at the level open to us and no level is too low. Each individual is an essential cog in the wheel of society, especially when he takes an active instead of a passive part.

No one ought to follow a certain path because it is what his wife prefers, or to impress his friends and neighbours, but because he has an inner compulsion – unless he is looking for stomach ulcers. No one should become a carpenter because it will please his mother, or because he is not cut out to be a scholar, but because his fingers itch to get hold of a hammer and chisel.

## STOP BEHAVING LIKE SHEEP

Human beings must stop behaving like sheep, they must cease being so utterly lacking in resourcefulness. Let us put the expression 'Stop the world I want to get off,' into practice. We can begin with the experts. They will without doubt not like it, but let us dispense with their documents, forms, quotations and conclusions for a whole week, and listen to what they have to say for themselves. What a lot of erroneous opinions would be replaced by common sense!

After this we can deal with the things that divert us. There will be no portable TV, games of cards or pop music to see us through the week, but some serious reading instead, and we shall get the world in perspective very quickly.

Next it is the turn of the housewife. She will forget her coffee breaks, her knitting and darning for a while and will occupy herself with all kinds of different pursuits like pottery, painting or toy-making. The business-man will do without his telephone, agendas and stockdealing and work in the kitchen or get out his tool box. Many people will look back on it as a lost week, but each of them stands a chance of 'coming to himself' and that is the object of the exercise. It may be that someone, somewhere, will not mind being seen doing something out of character any more.

Every moment of the day is an opportunity for performing some action in full consciousness of what we are doing. After all, we only live a moment at a time.

Why not begin with something extremely simple? Take a sip of tea, swill it round your mouth, savour it and let it slip down the throat. Well, well, you drank some tea! Break off a piece of bread, chew it, taste it, swallow it down and do absolutely nothing else for the time being. Find out for yourself what a beautiful experience it is. Then put on your coat, shut the front door behind you and you may succeed in living in a new dimension for the rest of the day.

Next day, begin just the same but as if you were doing it for the very first time; do it again the day after. All of a sudden you will become aware of yourself. You will feel the muscles in your buttocks as you sit down, the tightening in your mouth when you get angry. This is the instant when you remember yourself – when you notice your existence. You will see yourself crystal-clear and will know whether you have been rushing around too much or have been bone idle, whether you have been bringing on a headache or giving yourself piles, whether you are falling sick or keeping well.

**FLASHES OF INSIGHT**

Try to increase these flashes of insight. Say to yourself, 'I will remember myself three times a day. I will remember myself seven times a day. I will remember myself half a day.' Educate your attention at all costs. It is worth the trouble, because we learn to help ourselves and to distinguish between what does us good and what does not. On reading this, you may exclaim, 'If only it were so simple!' or perhaps, 'the writer is crazy!' Both comments are valid up to a point. Of course it is not simple, any more than it is simple to use one's foresight, to keep money from ruling our lives, to refrain from living a vicarious existence through other people, to avoid being so short-sighted. And, of course, I am crazy, in the sense in which I think we all ought to be crazy.

I am crazy from a worldly standpoint; but from a narrower standpoint I am not so crazy as might appear. Take a leaf out of my book. You can make yourself less sick, less unhappy, less disorientated and less aimless.

'Put the world right by making a start with yourself.' There it is once more, the dreaded cliché. What a pity it is not always put into practice. Take it easy to begin with. Be simple. Get to know what you eat, what you do, and think before you follow a trend.

CHAPTER TWELVE

# HERBAL TREATMENTS FOR COMMON AILMENTS

In conclusion, here are a few remedies for uncomplicated herbal treatment:

For *high blood-pressure* use a tea made of shepherd's purse, 1 oz (25g) of the fresh herb or 4 teaspoonsful of the dried to 1 pt ($\frac{1}{2}$l) of boiling water; allow to draw for 10 minutes, strain, and drink two cups per day.

For *rheumatism* drink an infusion of dried stinging nettles. The stinging nettle is rich in vitamin A and helps in infectious diseases. Pick the tops in spring and chop and sprinkle over soups (like chervil). Just dip the leaves in hot water to remove the sting. They are delicious, and indispensable as a blood-purifying course for the spring. The taste is marvellous. Eat stinging nettles for a month early in the year and you will not know the meaning of spring tiredness.

For *stones in the kidneys* drink a tea of young birch leaves, $\frac{1}{2}$ oz. (15g) for two cups. The flow of urine is increased and the uric acid is expelled. This is a very popular remedy in Finland and Russia.

For *insomnia* drink a tea of dill seed and chamomile.

For *gas in the intestines* drink an infusion of fennel seed – made like ordinary tea, but allowed to draw for 7 or 8 minutes and then strained. You will be relieved of wind very quickly.

For *arteriosclerosis* eat a few leaves of centaury every day.

For *constipation* eat a few leaves of dandelion every day. The chance is that it will visibly reduce piles (haemorrhoids) too.

For *depression* drink a tisane of Saint John's Wort. Both the leaves and the flowers are used. Boil up 4 teaspoonsful of the dried whole herb in a cup of water.

For *feverish colds and influenza* drink elder flower tea: three teaspoonsful of the dried herb in a cup of water, do not boil. Strain well after several minutes.

For a *fit of the blues* and general debility eat a few blades of plantain every day, they are packed with vitamin C.

This is only a brief mention of some of the innumerable herbs which are at our service, but it is a good start. If you are inclined to investigate, you will be very pleasantly surprised, and not simply by the flavours. You will find that I am telling the truth and, above all, that the various plants achieve considerably more than chemical pharmaceuticals do and often act very quickly into the bargain.

You will experience it personally and that is precisely what I am hoping.